Cornet Drake

Presented by

A. Adam Esq.

A MANUAL

FOR

VOLUNTEER CORPS

OF

CAVALRY.

LONDON:

PRINTED FOR THE WAR-OFFICE,

BY T. EGERTON, AT THE MILITARY LIBRARY, NEAR WHITEHALL.

1803.

Horse-Guards,
22d *November,* 1803.

THE following Instructions are recommended by His Royal Highness the COMMANDER IN CHIEF, for the use of the several Corps of Yeomanry and Volunteer Cavalry, throughout the United Kingdom.

By His Royal Highness's Command,

HARRY CALVERT,
Adjutant-General.

CONTENTS.

Sect.

1. *FORMATION of squadron and regiment*

GENERAL CIRCUMSTANCES REGULATING MOVEMENTS.

2. *Passaging and reining back*
3. *Dressing*
4. *Marching in front*
5. *Wheeling*
6. *Filing*
7. *Inclining*
8. *Pace*
9. *Of the charge or attack*
10. *Commands*
11. *Movements*
12. *Line of march and formation*
13. *Breaking and forming squadron*
14. *Open column in general*

CHANGES OF POSITION OF A REGIMENT.
Open Column.

15. ⎱ *Change of direction* ⎰ *On the reverse flank*
16. ⎰   ⎱ *On the pivot flank*
17. *March of rear divisions of a column into a new direction*

ON A FIXED POINT.

18. ⎫   ⎧ *Behind a placed flank division* —
19. ⎬ *Open column formed* ⎨ *Before a placed flank division* —
20. ⎭   ⎩ *Before and behind a central division*

CONTENTS.

Sect.

ON A DISTANT POINT.

21. ⎫
22. ⎪ Open column — ⎧ Changes position to a flank
23. ⎬   ⎪ Enters a line at its head point
24. ⎪   ⎨ Enters a line at its rear point
    ⎭   ⎩ Enters a line at a central point

25. Open column enters a line by the diagonal march of its divisions
26. Forms line by the divisions passing beyond each other

COUNTERMARCH.

27. Of each division separately
28. Of the divisions of the column from rear to front successively
29. Of squadron and regiment
30. Diminishing and increasing the front of the column

CLOSE COLUMN.

31. Close column formed from line
32. { The regiment forms close column ⎧ Before or behind a flank half squadron
                                      ⎨ On a central half squadron
                                      ⎩

33. ⎫ March of column ⎧ To a flank
34. ⎭   ⎩ To the front

35. { Change of direction in column ⎧ If halted
                                    ⎩ If on a march

36. Countermarch of the divisions of the column

37. Deployments into line ⎧ On the front half squadron —
                          ⎨ On the rear half squadron —
                          ⎩ On the central half squadron —

38. Oblique deployment ⎧ On a line advanced
                       ⎩ On a line retired

CONTENTS.

Sect.
39. *Line formed from column in the prolongation of its flank*
40. *Column of half distance forms line to its front*

ECHELLON.

41. *March of direct echellon to the front and formation in line*
42. *March in oblique echellon*
43. *Change of position on a fixed flank* { *When thrown forward / When thrown backward / On a central division* }

OF THE LINE.

44. *March in line*
45. *Advance of the line*
46. *Retreat of the line, and passage of obstacles*
47. *The line retires by alternate half squadrons Inversion of the line*
48. *When the commander of a line changes its position to a flank without the help of advanced objects*
49. *Passage of lines*
50. *Attack of cavalry to the front and flank*
51. *The column of route or march*

Evolutions
Inspection or review of a regiment of cavalry
Sword exercise
Movements and attacks
Additional instructions
Skirmishing
Advanced guards
Advanced posts
Patroles
Trumpet and bugle horn soundings
Words of command in movements and attacks

TABLE

EXPLAINING THE

SEVERAL FIGURES, MARKS, &c.

The STANDARD—denotes the Front.
POINTED ARROW—the Direction of the Movement.
DOTTED LINES—the March of different Bodies.
BLUNTED ARROW—the Markers neceſſary to determine the Wheel, &c. &c.
MOUNTED FIGURES—the new Direction and Poſition in Line.
SQUARE DOTS—Squadron Officers.
ROUND DOTS—Diviſion Leaders.

ABSTRACT

FROM

HIS MAJESTY's REGULATIONS

FOR THE

FORMATIONS AND MOVEMENTS

OF THE

C A V A L R Y.

S. 1. *Formation of Squadron and Regiment.*

THE Squadrons of cavalry are compofed each of two troops.

Regiments are compofed of two, three, or more fquadrons.

A Line is compofed of two or more regiments.

A fquadron formed in line with the files at fix inches from boot-top to boot-top, occupies in front nearly as many yards as it has files, or about thirty-four inches for each horfe.

In regiment or line, the fquadrons are formed with an interval betwixt each, equal to one third of their actual front.

All the various movements of the fquadron, or larger body, are compounded of *Paffaging* and *Reining back*—*Dreffing*—*Marching in front*—*Wheeling*—*Filing*—*Inclining*. {General movements of the fquadron.}

S. 2. *Paſſaging and Reining back.*

Paſſaging.
Paſſaging and reining back, are leſſons of the manage, and neceſſary in opening or cloſing of ranks, files, or intervals of ſquadrons.

When ground is to be taken to the flank by paſſaging, the whole body moves at the word To THE—— PASS! and halts at the word HALT! and therefore ſucceſſive movement of files is not to be permitted, nor will it be attempted if the command is given in a ſtrong and decided tone.

Reining back.
In reining back of bodies or ranks, the whole look to the hand to which they ought to form or dreſs; the movement is never to be hurried; to be made in order and the horſes to be kept ſtraight.

S. 3. *Dreſſing.*

Dreſſing.
Dreſſing is occaſional to right, center, or left, as ordered.

The ſquadron and all bodies till otherwiſe ordered,
- *Dreſs* — To the hand to which they form.
- *March* — To the hand to which they were dreſſed when halted.
- *Halt* — To the hand to which they were dreſſed when marching.

When the entire ſquadron moves in line, or wheels, *dreſſing* is to the ſtandard in the center.

When a column of entire ſquadrons marches in an alignement, in order to wheel up and form line, *dreſſing* and covering, as in other ſimilar columns, is to the pivot flank.

In *dreſſing* the horſes muſt ſtand ſtraight to the front, and the men's bodies muſt be ſquare, each juſt caſting his eye along his next man's face but without turning his head. The men muſt be uniformly placed on horſe-back, for on this ſquareneſs of man and horſe both dreſſing and movement moſt eſſentially depend.

All *dreſſing* is to be made with as much alacrity of officers

officers and soldiers as possible, and the dresser of each body as he accomplishes the operation will give a caution, *Front!* that heads may then be replaced and remain square to the front. If the body to be dressed is extensive, the dresser must justly place one division before he proceeds on that which is beyond it.

Every *dresser* of a body in a given line, must in his own person be placed on that line, while he is directing such operation.

S. 4. *Marching in Front.*

The squadron being supposed halted and dressed, the *leader* must take care that he is exactly placed before the standard, and square with respect to the front of the squadron, or the general line. In this position from habit, and with a glance of the eye, he determines the perpendicular direction which he is to follow, and cannot fail to remark two or more small objects on the ground, which are in the line of his direction.

Marching in line.

Line of march taken.

The leader gives the word, THE SQUADRON WILL ADVANCE! as a caution—at the word MARCH! each man casts his eyes to the standard, puts his horse in motion, and dresses with the greatest exactness to the standard, and non-commissioned officer that covers it.

Advance of the squadron.

The attention of the *standard-bearer* is to keep a horse's length from the leader, to follow him exactly and scrupulously, and slacken or quicken his pace according to the words of command or direction he receives. This must be done gradually, and without hurrying or springing forward, which will always occasion a shake in the squadron.

Attention of standard.

The attention of the rest of the squadron is invariably fixed on the center; that of the front rank on the standard; and that of the rear rank on the non-commissioned officer covering it, who gives the distance of ranks as ordered.

Attention of the ranks.

B 2   As

Attention of leaders of squadrons.

As the great business of every leader of a squadron is to carry it forward in its exact perpendicular direction, it requires his whole attention. The standard, officers, and serrefiles, must take care that the squadron is dressed, and up to its leader, who must not be looking back to give such directions, otherwise he will undoubtedly swerve, and not conduct it with that steadiness which is so essential, especially in relative movements, and which depend entirely upon himself.

Alteration of direction.

If a small alteration is to be made in the *direction* of the squadron, the leader gradually circles into such new direction, with which the squadron complies by advancing one flank and retaining the other, till the change is effected, and a straight line resumed.

Halt of Squadron.

When the word HALT! is given, the whole halt by the center. The word DRESS! instantaneously follows, and the file on each side of the standard diligently conforming to the general direction, gives the line to the rest of the squadron, who immediately, if necessary, correct the distance of files.

If one movement is immediately to succeed another, a critical dressing need not be required, and the squadron may remain looking to the center, till the order for marching is again given.

S. 5. *Wheeling.*

Wheeling.

WHEELING is one of the most essential and important operations of the squadron, necessary in many changes of position and in the formations of column and of the line.

Wheel of the squadron.

When the entire squadron is to wheel, a caution is given to that purport, and to which hand. At the word MARCH! the front rank of the squadron remains dressed to the center, the leader fixes his eye, and makes his circle on the standing flank man; the standard follows him exactly, and the squadron wheels with the same uniform front, at such a pace as is requisite to keep every where dressed with the standard.

The

The rear rank and the ferrefiles look to the wheeling flank, and incline at the same time that they wheel, so as always to cover their front leaders.

The *standard* must take care never to oblige the wheeling man to exceed a moderate gallop, otherwise the rear rank, which has still more ground to go over, cannot keep up, the squadron will wheel loose and in disorder, and be longer in dressing, than if it had come about at a slower pace, but close and connected. {Attention of standard.}

The *flanks* must always conform to the center, in case the leader does not take his ground as exactly as he ought. At any rate the standard is the guide for the pace, and to preserve the distance of files from. {Attention of the flanks.}

The leader must take care to time his words, HALT! DRESS! the instant before the wheel is compleated, otherwise an overwheel or reining back will be the consequence. The whole halt and dress by the center. {Halt of the squadron.}

In all division wheelings, the whole look to the wheeling hand. In all wheelings, the rear rank must rein back at the standing flank, and incline towards the wheeling hand in order to cover. {Rear rank.}

At the words, HALT! DRESS! given when the wheel is compleated, the whole turn eyes, and dress to the standing flank, and remain so until a new direction is given. {Halt of divisions.}

The distances of divisions of the squadron when in column, are taken and preserved from front rank to front rank. {Distances in column after wheeling.}

In division wheelings, the whole keep closed lightly towards the hand they wheel to, and must avoid pressing the pivot man off his ground. The outward flank man looks to his rank, he of course, regulates the pace at which the wheel is made, he must not press in on his rank, nor turn his horse's head towards the standing flank, all the horses heads must be kept rather outwards, (for to attempt to bend them inwards would certainly occasion a crowding on the standing flank), and the croupes lightly closed inwards with the leg. The pivot man of the wheel turns his horse on his forefeet, keeps his ground, and comes gradually round with his rank. {Attention in wheels of divisions.}

On a halted pivot.

Although in the completion of the wheel in column on a halted pivot, the pause made after the *halt!* *dress!* gives time in large fronts for exact dressing, before the *march!* is resumed; yet in small ones, where that pause is short, there is no time for such operation: the attention to, and preservation of the true distance, being then the material object. Whenever the wheel made is less than the quarter circle, the pause after the wheel will be considerable; should the wheel be greater than the quarter circle, it must be accelerated, otherwise more than one division will be arrived and arrested at the wheeling point.

On a moveable pivot.

When wheels or changes of direction of bodies in column, are made on a MOVEABLE PIVOT, both flanks are kept in motion, the *pivot* one always describing part of a circle, and the *reverse* flank, and intermediate men of the division, by a compound of inclining and wheeling, conforming to the pivot movement.

S. 6. *Filing.*

Filings.

FILING is an operation of the squadron, of use in broken or embarrassed ground, which will not allow of movements on a greater front. It is a situation in which horses move free and without confinement, but in which the squadron or its parts lengthen out, and take up much more ground than what they stand on in line; and is therefore to be had recourse to only from necessity.

Attentions in filing.

All horses heads are instantly to be turned at the command to *File!* ready to move off without loss of distance. The leaders of files go off short and quick, in their ordered direction, and are followed close by each man as it comes to his turn, so as to leave no unnecessary interval from one to another, and instantly to get off the ground. After being once in file, a distance of a yard from head to tail may be taken, so as to trot or gallop the easier if required. Every alteration of pace ought to be made as much as possible, by the whole at once;

once; if this is not obferved, a crowding and ftop in the rear will always attend fuch alteration.

The file leaders preferve fuch diftances as they ought, from which ever hand they are to drefs to, and the followers of each file are only attentive to cover, and be regulated by their proper file leaders. In file, the rear rank dreffes by, and is regulated by its front rank. Diftances when in file.

In forming, each man muft come up in file to his place, and by no means move up to his leader, till that leader has formed to which ever hand the file is forming to. The whole muft follow the exact tract of the firft leader, and come up one by one into their refpective places in fquadron. Attentions in forming.

Filings that may be required from the fquadron, are filing from either or both flanks, to front, flank, or rear, filing from the center of the fquadron to the front or to the flank. Filing fingle men by ranks, or by front and rear rank men alternately, from either flank of the fquadron. General and neceffary filing.

In the filings of the fquadron, the ferrefiles take their place in the rear of the files, unlefs the ground will allow them to remain on the flank of the rear rank; but their general and proper pofition, is in the rear of the files, becaufe filing is in general an operation of neceffity, which the nature of the ground requires. Serrefiles in filing.

S. 7. *Inclining.*

INCLINING is a movement, by which the fquadron is carried on in a parallel direction, at the fame time that it is gaining ground to the flank. It is of great ufe in the marching of the line in front, to correct any irregularities that may happen: it is equivalent to the oblique marching of the infantry. It enables to gain the enemy's flank, without expofing your own, or without wheeling or altering the parallel front of the fquadron. Inclining.

At the word to INCLINE! each man makes a half face on

on his horfe's fore feet, by which means, each will appear to be half a head behind his flank leader; and the whole will look to the hand to which they are to incline.

The leading officer on the flank, with a glance of his eye, afcertaining his points, marches fteadily upon them, at whatever pace is ordered. Every other man in the fquadron moves in fo many parallel lines, with refpect to him, and preferves the fame uniformity of front and file, as when he firft turned his horfe's head.

At no time of the incline, ought the former front of the fquadron, or diftance of files, to be altered. But whenever the word FRONT! is given, the fquadron (by each man at the fame inftant turning his horfe) fhould be formed in a direction perfectly parallel to its former front, and ready to drefs and move on by its ftandard.

The diftance of files, at fix inches, allows the fquadron to incline in perfect order, while its new direction does not pafs an angle of thirty-four degrees, with refpect to its former one; and at this angle it will be underftood always to incline; unlefs it fhould be required to gain as much or more ground to the flank, as to the front: in that cafe the fquadron muft either wheel up, and march upon the flank point, or it will fall more or lefs into file, according to the degree of obliquity required, by moving each horfe retired half neck, or head to boot.

S. 8. *Pace.*

THE *Walk! Trot!* and *Gallop!* are the three natural paces, and of each of thefe there are different degrees of quicknefs; but at which ever of them the fquadron is conducted, the floweft moving horfe at that pace muft be attended to, otherwife different kinds of motions will exift at the fame time in the fquadron, and tend to difunite it.

All alterations of pace muft be made as much as
poffible

poffible at the fame inftant, by each feparate body that compofes a line or column.

Though in flow movements of the line or fquadron, and on a march, the *Walk !* is the common pace ufed; yet in general, all changes of pofition and manœuvres, fhould be made at the *Trot !* or *Gallop !* according to circumftances, beginning gently to avoid hurry, and ending gently to avoid confufion in forming.

The intermediate times of fuch movement may be conducted with rapidity, and much depends on the eye of the officer, and well-timing the words of command.

S. 9. *Of the Charge or Attack.*

THE great force of cavalry is more in the offenfive than the defenfive, therefore the attack is its principal object. All the different movements of the fquadron fhould tend to place it in the moft advantageous fituation to attack the enemy.

The charge is that attack made with the greateft rapidity and regularity poffible, to break the order of the oppofite enemy, which will always enfure his defeat.

When the fquadron is to charge, the leader gives the words of command, MARCH! TROT! GALLOP! CHARGE! HALT! DRESS!

It depends on the commanding officer to lead at fuch a pace, as that the flanks and rear rank may always keep up. Every alteration of pace muft be made at the fame inftant by the whole fquadron.

Whatever diftance the fquadron has to go over, it may move at a brifk trot, till within two hundred and fifty yards of the enemy, and then gallop. The word CHARGE ! is given, when within eighty yards, and the gallop increafed as much as the body can bear in good order. Any attempt to clofe the files, at the inftant of the charge, would only increafe the intervals in a line,

line, and tend to impede the free movement of each horse, who at no time requires to be more independent than when galloping at his utmost exertion, and every rub to right or left diminishes that effort in a degree.

At the instant of the shock, the body must be well back, the horse not restrained by the bit, but determined forward by the spur; rising in the stirrups and pointing the sword, will always occasion a shake in the squadron; it will naturally be done when necessary.

It is in the uniform velocity of the squadron its effects consist; the spur as much as the sword tends to overset an opposite enemy; when the one has nearly accomplished this end, the other may complete it.

In every part of the charge and in quick movement, the standard must be very exact in following the leader, and the men particularly attentive in keeping up to, and dressing to their standard.

When the shock of the squadron has broken the order of the opposite enemy, part may be ordered to pursue and keep up the advantage, but its great object is instantly to rally, and to renew its efforts in a body, either to the front, or by wheeling to take other squadrons in flank.

A squadron should never be so much hurried, as to bring up the horses blown to the charge, and this will much depend on circumstances and the order they are in.

The regiment and squadrons must be well dressed before they move, horses perfectly straight, and carried on so during the whole of the attack, files on no account crowding; paces even and determined, horses in hand, and perfect attention and steadiness of every individual.

S. 10. *Commands.*

Command and duty of officers.

All COMMANDS must be given by officers, firm, loud, and explicit; every officer must therefore be accustomed to give such commands, even to the smallest bodies, in
the

the full extent of his voice. By such bodies he must not only be heard, but by the leaders of others who are dependent on his motions. The justness of execution and confidence of the soldier can only be in proportion to the firm, decided, and proper manner in which every officer of every rank gives his orders.

Commands of CAUTION, being such as are preparatory to a movement, should be sufficiently full and explanatory. Commands of EXECUTION should be short, and avoiding unessential words. Nature of commands

The commanding officers of regiments give and repeat all general commands, which are also shortly and quickly repeated by commanding officers of squadrons, especially such as MARCH! HALT! DRESS! It is only when the squadrons and line are broken into parts that the division officers give commands, and those chiefly executory, as HALT! DRESS! &c. also the several words necessary for the wheels made in column of march by each division, the several words necessary when the divisions come up successively from open or close column into line or column, whether conducted by line or flank movements, and in general whenever their divisions are moving as distinct though dependent bodies. But the wheeling from column into general line, or from line into general column, is made at the word MARCH! repeated by leaders of squadrons; the whole column is also put in march and halted by word from the leaders of squadrons, as is the squadron and regiment in all movements of the line in front. Commands given by respective leaders.

It is impossible to ascertain the words of command to be given in all cases; where such are not pointed out they must depend on the circumstances of the situation, and be short, clear, and expressive of what is to be done. All commands cannot be ascertained.

When a general order is not heard by a part of the line, each regimental commander (when the intention is obvious) will conform as quickly as possible to the movement which he sees executed on his right or left, according to the point from whence he perceives it to begin—but squadron and division officers execute only on the orders of their regimental commander. When commands are not distinctly heard.

After

Quick repetition of commands moſt eſſential.	After the chief commander has announced the orders, and particularly the words of execution, as MARCH! FORM! HALT! &c. the repetition of them by every other individual concerned muſt not be ſtrictly ſucceſſive, but as much as can be in a volley, to beget that preciſion of movement which in manœuvre is indiſpenſible; and the larger the body, the more eſſentially does this circumſtance operate.
Abbreviations of commands.	In the quick movements and manœuvres of cavalry there is not time for the full and formal words of command, on ſuch occaſions they muſt be rapidly given, much abridged, and all expletives omitted.

S. 11. *Movements.*

Diviſion of movements	MOVEMENTS muſt be divided into diſtinct parts, and each executed by ſeparate and explanatory words of command.
Alteration of poſition to begin from a Halt.	Alterations of poſition, in conſiderable bodies, muſt begin from a previous HALT! however ſhort; except giving a new direction to the heads of columns, or encreaſing or diminiſhing their fronts, which may be done while in motion. As the principle of moving, forming, and dreſſing, upon given and determined points is juſt, quick changes of poſition of a conſiderable body, formed in line, attempted while on the move, and not proceeding from a previous halt (however ſhort) will be falſe and defective; the effects of which, though not ſo apparent in a ſingle ſquadron or regiment, would be very obvious in a line or column of any extent. A pauſe between each change of ſituation, ſo eſſentially neceſſary to the movements of great bodies, ſhould ſeldom be omitted in thoſe of ſmall ones; ſquareneſs of dreſſing, the exact perpendiculars of march, and the correct relative poſition of the whole are thereby aſcertained. Such alterations of ſituation made from the halt may, when neceſſary, ſucceed each other inſtantly and quickly; no time need be taken up in ſcrupulous dreſſing,

fing, but every one may be immediately apprized of the following movement which circumftances require.

In the movements of a SINGLE Regiment, and in the taking up of a new pofition, it may not feem material whether a flank of it is placed a few yards to the one hand or other, or whether the line formed on is exactly directed on any certain point.—But when a regiment makes a part of a more confiderable body, then all its pofitions being relative to other regiments and to given points, if its formations are not accurate and juft, it will create general confufion, and give falfe directions and diftances to thofe whofe fituations may be determined by it.

Neceffity of preci-
fion in the movements of fingle regiments.

The neceffity of every fingle regiment being accuftomed to make its changes of pofition and formation on determined points, is therefore obvious, and to which they fhould be carefully trained.

If OFFICERS are obferving of, and attentive to their true diftances of divifions, and of the covering of their pivot flanks, the moft confiderable column of cavalry ought to be able in changing its pofition, to ENTER on a given alignement, at a brifk TROT;—To HALT!— To WHEEL INTO LINE!—To ADVANCE!—And to CHARGE!—without more than a momentary paufe between each operation of the halt, wheel and advance, and without being under any neceffity of dreffing, correcting diftances, or alteration whatever.

What is required of a line of cavalry.

Although the nature of Routes and of Roads may fometimes limit common marches to be made on a very fmall front, yet flank marches near an enemy, or changes of pofition in the prefence of an enemy, cannot be effected with precifion, firmnefs, or certainty, on a lefs front than *ranks by threes*, or indeed when poffible on a front of a *divifion* (or of a *fub-divifion*, if the fquadron is ftrong as from forty eight to fixty files) for then the fteadinefs and correctnefs of pivot officers may enfure the inftant HALT!—WHEEL INTO LINE!—and ADVANCE!—upon the enemy.—And it will feldom happen

Movements in column if poffible to be made by divifions or fub-divifions.

happen that changes of pofition made in order to attack to the greater advantage will be required; but in fituations that allow fuch changes to be made by a flank movement, and without lengthening out the line during the tranfition from one point to another.

S. 12. *Line of March and Formation.*

Movements in a ftraight line always made on two objects

Every LEADER of a body, moving on any front whatever, who means to conduct it in a ftraight line, muft march upon *two* points, which he invariably preferves fo as to cover each other; if fuch points are not afcertained for him he muft inftantly determine them for himfelf, and if no ftrong or marked objects prefent themfelves in his direction, he can never fail by cafting his eyes along the ground, to find fuch fmall ones as will anfwer his purpofe, and thefe from time to time he renews as he approaches them.—To march ftraight on one object only with certainty and without wavering is not to be depended on.

The alignement

To march or form in the *alignement*, is to make troops march and form in any part of the ftraight line which joins two given points, or is prolonged beyond them.

Taking up a line of formation.

The *line* on which troops in column move ftraight, or on which they are fucceffively to form, is taken up to an extent by the prolongation of an original, fhort, and given *bafe* of two perfons placed where the troops begin firft to enter, or form upon that line; the direction of which has been determined by the views of the commander, and which can feldom fail to point on fome diftant and diftinct object, that will ferve to correct the pofition of the different perfons who fucceffively, as their feparate bodies require it, prolong the line from the feveral points already eftablifhed in it.

Pofition of markers of the line.

When the leading body of a column arrives at any point where it is to enter on a ftraight line, a perfon will be placed with his horfe's head facing to the pivot flank
of

of the column; each leader will thus know why he is so placed, and will, in passing close to him and to every other person posted in a similar manner, give every attention to continue the alignement.

Ascertaining the points necessary for the movements and formations of the regiment, is the particular business of the adjutant in the field; in this exercise he may be assisted by detached persons placed behind each flank, who are properly trained quickly to take up such line as he shall give them; and for this purpose they are only to be sent out successively, and as their aid is wanted, nor are they to make any bustle or unnecessary parade; and when the operation for which they are sent out is accomplished, they will return immediately behind their proper flank.

Points of movement and formation ascertained by appointed persons.

The necessity of officers and non-commissioned officers being well trained, to prolong lines, take up distances, and give those aids which are so essential in the formations and movements of all considerable bodies, is evident, and much to be attended to. Persons active, intelligent, and well mounted, can alone assist the operations of cavalry, nor are camp colours, nor any such improper and superfluous modes necessary, or in general to be used.

The necessity of persons well trained to prolong and give line of march and formation.

The markers of the alignement in column, or of the formations in line, are not to quit their ground after the halt of either, till all necessary dressing is accomplished, and that they are directed so to do; they serve not only as points of movement, but as points of correction.

S. 13. *Breaking and forming Squadrons.*

When the squadron has wheeled to a flank by *half squadrons*, by *divisions*, or by *sub-divisions* of more than six files, it then occupies less ground than it before stood on, by the front of the column, whatever it is.

Whenever

Leaders of divisions of the squadron.

Whenever the SQUADRON is broken into divisions, or parts, for the purpose of movement, each separate body has a leader, on whom the eye and attention of each soldier is fixed. In *column* such leader will be on the pivot flank of his division in all situations of manœuvre. These leaders cover each other in the given direction in which the column is to move; they are not themselves then to be covered by any one, and are answerable for true distances. Should any such leader not be appointed, or be wanting to a division, his place is to remain vacant, and not to be occupied by the flank files of men, for such flank files of men are invariably to remain covering each other.

Commands given when the squadron breaks to a flank by any of its tellings off.

When from the halt, the squadron, by wheels to its flank, *breaks into open column*, the commanding officer gives the words (HALF SQUADRONS, DIVISIONS, SUBDIVISIONS) TO THE { Right or Left } WHEEL! MARCH! HALT! DRESS! by the standing flank, and then EYES { Right or Left } by the pivot flank; after which the whole is put in motion by the word MARCH! Should the word EYES (right or left) be omitted, at any rate they are directed to the pivot flank, at the word MARCH!

Pivot leaders in column of half squadrons.

When the squadron has wheeled to a flank by *half squadrons*. If *to the right*, the officer from the right of the squadron immediately shifts to the left of his half squadron, to conduct the pivot of the leading half squadron, and the officer who was on the left of the squadron wheels up, and remains on the pivot of his own half squadron. *If to the left*, then the left officer shifts to the right of his half squadron, and the right officer wheels up, and remains on the right of his own half squadron.

Standard in column.

In the wheelings of the squadron into *half squadrons, divisions*, or *sub-divisions*, the standard and its coverer wheel up with the leading half squadron, or the second division, or the fourth sub-division from the flank wheeled to, to, so as to place themselves, at the conclusion of the wheel, behind the second and third file from the pivot of each of the said bodies. And when these bodies wheel up to form squadron, the standard shifts briskly to its place in the center during the wheel.

When from the halt the squadron wheels to its flank, *ranks by three's* or by *two's*, the commanding officer gives the words (RANKS BY THREE'S OR BY TWO'S) TO THE $\left\{ \begin{array}{c} \text{Right} \\ \text{or} \\ \text{Left} \end{array} \right\}$ WHEEL! MARCH! HALT! DRESS! to the pivot hand, after which the whole is put in motion at the second word MARCH! the whole three's at the same time, and increasing their distances while on the move; or the two's (who are standing at a half wheel) successively, as soon as each is enabled so to do, and can get its marching distance. *Commands given when a squadron wheels to a flank ranks by three's or by two's.*

When the squadron wheels to the right or left, by *ranks by three's*, the middle man of each three will turn on his horse's fore feet; and of the other two, one will rein back, and the other moves forward to dress with him. A flank officer is at the head of the squadron, the other flank officer at the rear. The standard is in the middle of the leading center rank of fixes when wheeled up, and its coverer is in the middle of the rank behind it. The supernumeraries of the rear rank will, if the ground requires it, fall in and follow the rear of the squadron, or otherwise turn singly, and march on its flank. In this situation in movement, the squadron has opened out one sixth more than the ground it stood formed on. *Column of ranks by three's.*

When the squadron wheels to a flank, by *ranks by two's*, the flank man of each two will half turn on his horse's fore feet, and the other man will half wheel up, so as to make a half face to the flank, and be in a situation to move off successively as it comes to their turn. A flank officer is at the head of the squadron, the other flank officer in the rear of it. The standard and its coverer turn each on his own ground, and move between the ranks; the serrefiles of the rear will, if the ground requires it, fall in and follow the rear of the squadron, *Column of ranks by two's.*

C or

or otherwife turn fingly, and march on its flank. In this fituation in movement, the fquadron has opened out near two thirds more than the ground it ftood formed on.

Serrefiles in column.
When, for the purpofe of *manœuvre*, the fquadron breaks to the flank by half fquadrons or divifions, the ferrefiles are clofe up behind each; when by fub-divifions, they are on the flank, not the pivot one.

Halts of divifions.
Halts of divifions from wheels, are made with eyes turned to the ftanding flank.

Poft of commanding officers.
Commanding officers of regiments and fquadrons remain on (but wide of) the pivot flanks, to obferve and regulate the march, and inftantaneoufly to form when ordered.

Shifting of officers to pivot flanks.
Commanding officers muft take care that conducting officers of flanks or pivots fhift nimbly to fuch points, at the proper inftant they fhould there place themfelves.

Formation of the fquadron and line from column of divifions.
If a line has marched to a flank in *column of fquadrons, half fquadrons, divifions*, or *fub-divifions*, in fuch cafes it occupies (intervals being preferred) exactly the ground requifite for its formation in line; which is at any inftant made by halting, and wheeling up the quarter circle.

Formation of the fquadron and line from column of ranks by three's.
If a line is moving to a flank, fquadrons by *ranks by three's*. As each fquadron in march then occupies more ground than what it ftands on when formed, and that about half the intervals ftill ought to remain, therefore if the whole halts at the fame inftant, and *each* fquadron wheels up its three's clofing them at the fame time to its leading flank, the line fhould then be completely formed with its proper interval. The fquadrons thus forming all at the fame time.

Formation of the fquadron and line from column of ranks by two's.
If a line is marching correctly to the flank, *ranks by two's*, every man as clofe as he well can to his preceding file leader, no diftance between fquadrons, that it halts, and that the pivot men are covered, fuch line will ftill have lengthened out confiderably, viz. one third at leaft. Therefore, if it forms to the pivot flank, the four leading men of the head fquadron wheel up to the flank by two's;

two's; the other men of the leading squadron successively wheel up when they close to their respective leaders; each other squadron, as its head arrives at its interval distance from the preceding one, halts and forms in the same manner. The squadrons thus form successively as they gain their distances.

When from the halt, and from open column, the squadron is formed by the *wheeling up of its divisions*. The commanding officer gives the words (Half Squadrons, Divisions, Sub-Divisions, Ranks by Three's) WHEEL INTO LINE! on which pivot leaders immediately place themselves on the reverse flank of such division, as by its wheel up brings them to their true place in the squadron; the pivot officer of the rear division is alone an exception, being already at his post in squadron. At the word MARCH! the whole wheel up, and receive the word HALT! DRESS! by the standing flank, and the line of pivots; the standard, serrefiles, and every thing having resumed their place in squadron. Squadrons forming from ranks by *two's*, receive successively from their leaders, as their heads come to their ground, the words, WHEEL INTO SQUADRON! HALT; DRESS! to the hand formed to.

When the column of — wheels up into squadron or line.

In wheeling from column into line, it is on the *flank files of men*, and not on the pivot leaders that the wheels are made; therefore, at the word being given to WHEEL INTO LINE! those leaders quit the flanks, and are disposed of as above, and this allows that after the wheel the horses heads of the pivot men exactly touch the heads of those that are facing towards and marking the general line.

Wheels from column into line made on pivot files of men.

When the open column of squadrons stands halted, ready to *wheel up into line*, on the caution so to do, and before the word MARCH! an officer or under officer from the wheeling flank (or from the rear) of each squadron, moves quickly forward, and places himself in the line of pivots, and thereby becomes an object, which determines the square of the wheel, and which the outward man of each squadron knows he is not to pass. In an open column of half squadrons, the leading half only of each squadron will send out such an object, as

Aids necessary to be given when the column moves up into line.

the rear half (if diſtances are juſt) wheels up to the pivot of the leading half. In an open column of diviſions, or ſub-diviſions, the leading one of each will only ſend out ſuch object. In column of ranks by three's, or by two's, commanding officers of regiments will always endeavour by detached perſons, to prolong the line as taken from the head of the column, in order to make their reſpective formations correct in the general line. The rear diviſion of a column, before it wheels up into line, will always place an object of formation behind its pivot flank, and ſuch object is the one on which the flank ſquadron is corrected after the wheel into line.

S. 14. *Open Column.*

Formation of columns

ALL COLUMNS are ſuppoſed formed from line, for the convenience of movement, and for the purpoſe of again extending into line. Every column of march or manœuvre muſt be formed by a regular ſucceſſion of the diviſions from one flank to the other of the line, or of ſuch of its parts as compoſe the column, for whatever is the relative poſition of a body in line, ſuch ought it to be in column; and where ſeveral connected columns are formed, the ſame flanks of each ſhould be in front; but whether rights or lefts will depend on circumſtances. Columns formed from the center of regiments or lines will ſeldom be made, are partial, and not adapted as the others are to movements, and formations in all ſituations.

Columns of march and manœuvre.

The column is named that of *march*, or *route*, when applied to common marches, where the attention of men and officers is not ſo much kept on the ſtretch. It is named the *column of manœuvre*, when being within reach of an enemy, the greateſt exactneſs is required, in order to its ſpeedy formation at any inſtant into line during its tranſition from one poſition to another.

Front and extent of columns.

Columns of march or manœuvre will be compoſed of diviſions, ſub-diviſions, or ranks by three's; for the purpoſes of movement they need not exceed twelve file in front, nor should they be under six men in front, otherwise there will not be space to loosen the ranks, and the line will be of course lengthened out, as happens in the march of ranks by two's or by files. From six to ten men in front are most advantageously composed for quick manœuvres.

Columns of march or manœuvre will be formed with the left in front, whenever it is probable that the formation of the line will be required to the right flank, and *vice versa* when required to the left flank.

<small>Circumstances determine the leading flank of columns.</small>

The proper pivot flank in column, is that which, when wheeled up to, preserves the divisions of the line in the natural order, and to their proper front; the other may be called the *reverse flank*. In column, divisions cover and dress to the proper pivot flank ; to the left when the right is in front, and to the right when the left is in front.

<small>Pivot flank and reverse flank of divisions, &c. in column.</small>

In column the chief commander is with the leading division, and in line with the directing squadron.

In all movements, formations, and changes of position of the column, *distances and dressing* are taken from the directing hand, viz. from the head of the column, or from the hand to which the formation is making, or to be made.

<small>Distances and dressing where taken from.</small>

In column, the *pivot officers*, or non-commissioned officers, are answerable for covering, and for proper wheeling distances, and the eyes of the whole are turned to the pivot; such pivot leaders must attend to those two circumstances only, and by no means be looking to or giving directions to their divisions; that care must be left to the officers on the other flank, or in the rear ; for if they themselves move steadily and truly, there is little doubt but their divisions will always keep up to them.

<small>Pivot Officers.</small>

The rear divisions of a column in march always follow every turn and twist which the head makes ; each successively changing its direction at whatever point the leading one may have so done. When at an unexpected moment a column is ordered to halt, the pivot leaders of each

<small>Attention of the rear divisions of the column when in march.</small>

each divifion muft remain fixed where they are found, at the word HALT. If the march of the column is again to be refumed, the rear divifions will continue to follow the exact path traced out by the head; nor are any of the following divifions of a column ever to deviate from this rule, or endeavour of themfelves to get into a ftraight line, when the general direction is a winding one, until an exprefs order is given for that purpofe, which can hardly ever happen, till the head of the column is halted, with a determination to form the line in a ftraight direction, in which cafe the correction of pivots will begin from the head of the column.

<small>Commander and Adjutant of a regiment correct pivots.</small>

In column, the commander of a regiment remains near its leading divifion, and the adjutant (or fome appointed perfon) remains near its clofing divifion; they are thus ready to preferve the line of march, and at the inftant of halting, to make fuch correction of pivots as may be neceffary; for which purpofe the adjutant takes care immediately to place himfelf in the prolongation of the general line, which he takes up from the points in his front already eftablifhed in it, and from fuch bodies as before him have already halted in it. In this manner the adjutant in his own perfon gives the flank point on which each commander from his leading divifion at all times forms and dreffes his fquadron and regiment.

<small>The front of column not to be altered when marching in an alignement</small>

No doubling up, encreafing, or diminifhing the front of the Column, muft be made after entering on a ftraight alignement in order to form in line; fuch operation, when neceffary, fhould be performed before the line of formation is entered on.

<small>Correction of pivots of open column before wheeling into line.</small>

When the open column has marched on in an alignement, and is ordered to halt and form line, the pivots of the leading regiment are immediately corrected if neceffary, the others inftantly perfect their line upon it, and upon each other, and no time is loft in wheeling up into line and then advancing.

<small>Correction of the fquadron and of the line af-</small>

If the regiment, after wheeling up from column into line, is not critically well dreffed, the fault muft be in the internal part of the divifions; this muft be immediately

diately corrected by each squadron leader on his former pivot men, who on no account must have moved; but remain so many fixed points, on whom the whole are lined. If any farther dressing is necessary, it is ordered and made by a field officer, who himself moves quickly close along the front from the flank to which eyes are turned, to the other flank. *ter wheeling up from a column.*

A column in movement should, if possible, never occupy more ground than what it stands on in line: but when the formation into line must undoubtedly be to the front, then the divisions may be ordered to march closed up to half, quarter, or any other distance, and the formation may be made by prolonging the line, by deployment, by inclining up, or by half wheels, and marching in the oblique lines, as circumstances require. *Necessary extent of a column of march.*

Columns marching at half or quarter distance of their then front must also make their necessary wheels on a *moveable* pivot, otherwise a stop must ensue, and a column open out.

In all wheels of a column, in movement to change direction, and made by divisions on a *fixed* flank, the outward file, whether officer or man, is the one wheeled upon; and the quickness of the wheels must at least be double to the rate of march, otherwise the column may be liable to open out, and the wheeling point would not be cleared in time for each successive division. In changes made on a *moveable* flank, the outward file of that flank is also the directing one. *Quickness of wheels in column.*

Halts of divisions from wheels are made with eyes turned to the standing flank. But all *halts* from a march in front are made with the eyes turned to the point or points to which the troops while in march are looking. After which, no dressing or movement whatever is to be made, until a separate order directs it. *Halting from the wheel or from march.*

The whole column or line should always be in so correct a situation, as to halt instantly on the word HALT! But *The halt of the line or column,*

But should, at any time, the difficulties of the ground have unavoidably opened out the column, or thrown squadrons out of the line, in such case the halt of those squadrons will be successive, as they regain their proper situations.

Deployments, &c. made by ranks by three's.

When squadrons, half squadrons, or divisions, separately move by a flank, to change position in column, or from line to place themselves in open or close column, or from close column to deploy into line, &c. it will always, when possible, be done by *ranks by three's*, and the greatest care be given, that the three's move as close as they can, that at the instant the word HALT! FRONT! is given to each, the division may be exactly formed by the wheeling of its three's, without any necessity of a closing in of its rear.

Post of commanding officers of each regiment.

The commanding officers of regiments are in the charge at the head of one of their squadrons, generally of the one nearest that of direction. In all other situations of manœuvre they are moveable according to circumstances, in general near the head of their column, or of their body, which first forms in line; when the line is formed in parade, they are at the head of their right squadron.

CHANGES OF POSITION OF A REGIMENT.

OPEN COLUMN.

S. 15. When the Open Column wheels on its halted reverse Flank into a new Alignement, and marches on it.

CAUTION TO { The new alignement being determined by placed objects, and the point of entry being marked, the leading officer who has marched his

Right wheel!	his pivot flank on that point, when he arrives at a distance equal to the front of his division from it, orders (right or left) *wheel!* (according to whatever is the reverse flank); and the wheel is made so that on the conclusion of it, at the word, *Halt, Dress!* he himself shall be placed on the new alignement on the pivot of his division, ready to give the word *March!* as soon as the succeeding division has arrived at the wheeling point.
Halt, Dress!	
March!	
Wheel!	The officer of the Second division gives the word *Wheel!* when he arrives at the ground which the first is quitting, and then *Halt! Dress!* when the wheel is completed; in this situation he remains till he perceives the preceding division has gained from him a distance equal to the front of his division, he then instantly gives the word *March!* and follows in column. Each succeeding division observes the same directions, and the equality of pace being preserved, the column may continue its march in perfect order.
Halt, Dress!	
March!	

S. 16. *When the Open Column wheels on its halted pivot Flank into a new Alignement, and marches in it.*

CAUTION.	The leading division begins its wheel to the pivot flank on the alignement itself, when its pivot flank officer arrives at the point of wheeling
Left, Wheel!	
Halt, Dress!	

March!	wheeling, inſtead of (as in the preceding ſection) beginning at the diſtance of a diviſion ſhort of that point.

S. 17. *When Part of the Open Column halts in the new Direction, and the remaining Diviſions are ordered to enter by flank Marching.*

HALT!	When the head of a regimental column arrives at a given point, the whole is ordered to HALT! Such diviſions of the column as are ſtill in the old direction are then ordered to WHEEL to their pivot flank ranks by three's—They MARCH! and ſucceſſively place their pivots on the new line at their juſt wheeling diſtances, which are aſcertained for them by the perſons they timeouſly detach for that purpoſe. The whole pivots being thus covered and dreſſed in the new direction, the column is prepared for wheeling into line.
THREE'S, RIGHT WHEEL! MARCH! *Halt, Dreſs!* MARCH! *Halt,—Wheel up! Halt, Dreſs!*	

ON A FIXED POINT.

S. 18. *When the Regiment forms Open Column of Diviſions behind a placed Flank Diviſion, and throws back the other Flank.*

Two perſons are advanced immediately before the flank diviſion to mark, and who face to the determined line on which the pivots of the column are to ſtand.

The

Caution.	The flank division is *placed* perpendicular to that line, and with its pivot upon it.
Divisions, Right wheel! March! Halt, Dress!	The line Wheels up into open column of similar divisions, towards the placed division.
Three's, Right wheel! March! Halt, Dress!	The divisions having wheeled the quarter circle, each breaks ranks by three's, the reverse and not the pivot flank leading, and the conductor being there placed.
March! Halt! Wheel up! Halt, Dress!	The divisions March! and form in open column behind the head division and each other, preserving their wheeling and interval distances, and placing their pivot flanks on the new line, which is taken from the original objects in it, and prolonged to each of them by their own detached persons. The *pivots* being covered and dressed, and distances just from front to rear of the column, the whole is in a situation to *wheel* into line.

The better to ascertain those flank points, the coverer of each pivot leader will successively, as they approach the new line, gallop on and place himself upon it at the wheeling distance of his division from the one before him, facing to the head of the column, and covering exactly those that have already taken their places therein —The coverer thus standing on the spot which his leader is afterwards to occupy, such and every other leader, when he arrives

Halt! Wheel up!
Halt, Dress!

rives at the line, stops there himself, allows his division to pass on behind its marker, till its *rear* comes up; he then *Halts, Fronts* it, and *dresses* and closes it to its pivot marker on the line. It is to be observed, that in this case the divisions *cross* the new line, in order to place their pivots upon it.

All divisions that by flank marching mean to form in open column on a new line, should take particular care that the last part of their movements, and at least for a space equal to their own extent, is made in a line not oblique, but square and perpendicular to the line of pivots, for thereby they will at once form up firm, compact, and on their true ground; and therefore in the first part of their march, the head of their divisions should not be directed on their future pivot point, but rather wide of it, so as to allow for the square entry of each on its forming ground.

If when from line, divisions wheel into open column towards a standing division, and the flanks of the division next such standing one may not thereby be sufficiently disengaged for whatever movement is immediately to be required, such division (alone) may be ordered only to half wheel, quarter wheel, or rein back a flank, as may best answer the proposed end.

S. 19. *When the Regiment forms Open Column of Divisions before a Flank Division, and throws forward the other Flank.*

Two persons are placed behind the flank division, in order to give the determined line on which the pivots of the column are to stand, as directed in the preceding movement.

The

CAUTION.	The *flank* division by wheeling, or countermarching, is placed with its pivot on, and perpendicular to that line, and in such situation it makes front towards the rear.
DIVISIONS, RIGHT WHEEL! MARCH! HALT, DRESS!	The line wheels up into open column of divisions towards the placed division.
THREE'S, LEFT WHEEL! MARCH! *Halt, Dress!*	The divisions having wheeled the quarter circle, each goes ranks by three's, the pivot flank leading.
MARCH! *Halt! Wheel up! Halt, Dress!*	The divisions MARCH and form open column as before—In this case, as their pivot flanks lead, they do not *cross* the new line, but arrive at and place them upon it; the pivot leader himself there remaining. The pivots being covered and distances just, the column stands ready to WHEEL into line, or to march on.

S. 20. *When the Regiment forms open Column of Divisions, before and behind a central Division.*

The *central* division is named, and also the wings, as they are to be before or behind it.

The *new* direction is taken, and the central division placed.

CAUTION! DIVISIONS WHEEL INWARDS! MARCH! HALT, DRESS!	The line is ordered to WHEEL inwards by divisions of squadron towards the placed division, and thus stands in two open columns facing each other.

The

THREE's, RIGHT WHEEL! MARCH! *Halt, Drefs!* MARCH!	The divifions WHEEL ranks by threes, both to the fame flank, viz. their leading one, which in thofe that are to move to the front is the *pivot* flank, and in thofe that are to move to the rear, is the *reverfe* flank.
HALT! WHEEL UP! *Halt, Drefs!*	The part of the line, which leads with its reverfe flank, forms in column *behind* the placed divifion, the part which leads with its pivot flank forms in column *before* the placed divifion; and its head divifion is to remember, that if the line is afterwards to be formed, it will take a double wheeling diftance from the divifion it fronts, as they would then wheel up towards each other; but if the column is to move on, it will take only fingle diftance.

In this formation the *pivot* line fhould be fufficiently marked by detached perfons, both before and behind the central divifion, and the pivots of the wing, which forms behind it, will take their general direction from the pivots of thofe that form before it, as thefe laft have the greateft facility in forming in confequence of their pivot flanks leading.

When the *whole* are thus in column, facing the central divifion, if the line is to be formed, the whole will WHEEL up to their pivots—If the column is to march, the neceffary part of it will COUNTERMARCH its divifions, and then the whole can move on.

ON

ON A DISTANT POINT.

S. 21. *When the Regiment changes to a distant Position in Front or Rear, by the Flank marching of the open Column, and that this Position is either parallel or oblique to the one it quits.*

Divisions—
Wheel! March!
Halt, Dress!

{ The regiment breaks into open column of divisions to whichever hand the new position out-flanks the old one, for to that hand will the whole have to incline during the march; and if it does not sensibly out-flank, then the regiment will break to the hand next to the point of intersection of the two lines, for that hand is nearest to, and will, in general, be the first to enter any part of the new position.

Threes—wheel!
March!
Halt, Dress!

{ The regiment standing in open column is ordered to WHEEL its divisions by *three's* to a flank. The leader of the second division has then a direction given him, which crosses the new line at the point, as near as can be judged, where the flank of that division is to be placed. The whole are then put in motion. The leader

March!

of the second division marches in his given direction at a steady pace; the commander of the regiment remains with the head division, and by making it gradually advance or keep back, regulates the heads of all the others during the march, as they endeavour to continue themselves nearly in the prolonged line of the heads

of

Halt! Wheel up!
Halt, Dress!

of the two leading divisions; but at any rate they are not to be before them: and when these two divisions *halt* their pivots in the line, the others, without hurrying, arrive successively in the new direction, and stand in open column at their just wheeling distances. When the head of the column is within sixty or seventy yards of the new line (its direction being already prepared) the pivot markers gallop out, and mark the pivot flanks of their several divisions.

In this manner the commander, who is himself with and conducts the two leading divisions, moves them in the direction that best answers his views, and at once takes up any position, and to any front that is necessary. As circumstances change his intentions, he may at every instant, vary and direct them upon new points of march, the other divisions of the column conforming (without the necessity of sending particular orders) to whatever alterations of direction the head may take; and the commander conducting that head so as to enable the rear to comply with its movements without hurry. During the transition, the wheeling distances should be nearly preserved by the divisions; but at any rate great care must be taken that they are correct, just before entering the new line.

S. 22. When the Regiment changes Position, by breaking into open Column of Divisions or Half Squadrons, marches to the Point in a new Line where its Head is to be placed, and enters on the Line by the Flank March of Divisions.

The pivot flank of the column being directed on the person who marks

Halt!	marks the flank point in the new line, the whole will Halt when arrived within a few yards of him; and a point of direction 60 or 70 yards beyond is supposed also to be ascertained.—The divisions are then wheeled by three's, (to the right or left as is necessary to conduct into the new line) and the pivot markers move out to mark their points for each division.
Three's —— Wheel! March! Halt! Dress!	
March! Halt! Wheel up! Halt, Dress!	At the word March! the whole divisions move by their flanks; the head one places its pivot at a wheeling distance from the person, and every other one in the manner before directed, arrange themselves behind the head one, and behind each other; their flanks being corrected by the commanding officer, they are then ready to *wheel* up into line.

The flank which the divisions *break* to by *three's*, and move from, will depend on which side of the person they are to be arranged, and which way the line is to face.

S. 23. *When the Regiment changes Position by breaking into open Column of Divisions, or Half Squadrons, marching to the Point in the new Line, where its rear is to be placed, and entering on and prolonging the Line, by the successive Wheels of its Divisions.*

Besides the person who marks the point of *entry*, two advanced points of march must be given. The column then enters by the successive wheels of its divisions and

Halt!	and moves on, and when its laſt diviſion is at its point, it receives the word Halt! and pivots being correded, the whole are ready to wheel up into line.

S. 24. *When the Regiment changes Poſition by breaking into open Column, marching to the Point in the new Line, where a central Diviſion is to be placed, and there entering on the Line.*

—— *Wheel!* *Halt, Dreſs!* *March!* Halt!	The leading diviſion of the column having at the given point *wheeled* into the alignement, followed by the others as far as the named central diviſion; the word Halt! is then given, and the column ſtops.
Three's! —— Wheel! March! Halt! Dress!	Such diviſions as have already wheeled into the new alignement, being now at their proper points, remain ſo.—Such diviſions as are ſtill in the old direction, are ordered to wheel by three's, to the flank which conducts to their place in the new line, and the markers move forward.
March! *Halt!* *Wheel up!* *Halt! Dreſs!*	At the command to March! they all move on, and *halt* with their pivot flanks on it, ready to Wheel up into line.

This movement includes both the operations of a regiment, as entering a new line, where its rear is to reſt, and where its front is to reſt.

S. 25. *When the Regiment changes Position by breaking into open Column, marching to the Point in the new Line, where its head Division is to be placed, and on which its rear Divisions form by the Diagonal March of each.*

Halt!	The column will advance to the spot where its leading division is to be placed, and will then receive the word Halt! The leading division will then more accurately be placed on the new line; and each of the other divisions will be ordered to Wheel back on its reverse flank, as much as is necessary to place that flank perpendicular to its point in the new line. The conducting officers having placed themselves on that flank, the whole will March and successively form up to the leading division by the diagonal movement. In this manner the divisions of the column arrive in full front, one after another, in the new line; and that line must face the same way the column did.
On the —— rein back!	
March!	
Halt, Dress!	
March!	
—— *Shoulder forward! Forward! Halt, Dress!*	

If the column halts perpendicular to the new line, its divisions will wheel back one eighth of the circle, or a half wheel.—If the column halts oblique to the new line, the divisions will proportionally wheel so as to be placed perpendicular to their future lines of march.

S. 26. *When the open Column halts and forms in Line to the leading Division, and facing either to the Front or Rear, by the Divisions successively passing behind the leading one, and each other.*

Halt!

> The column arrives in the direction of, or in any direction oblique or perpendicular behind the line, and Halts.—The leading division either remains on its ground, or wheels to its reverse flank, or wheels about on its reverse flank, according to the position to be taken.

March!
—— *Wheel!*
Halt! Dress!
March!

—— *Wheel!*
Halt! Dress!
March!
Halt! Dress!

> All the pivot leaders place themselves on the *reverse* flank of the divisions, and eyes are turned to them.—The head division standing fast, the others are put in *motion*, and each division successively *wheels*, and passes close behind the head division, and again *wheels* when opposite its place, *marches* up and *halts* to the standing part of the line, which is properly prolonged for the correction of their dressing.

The divisions thus successively come into line, making their wheels rapidly and sharp, so as not to impede the following of the column.

This formation occurs when the direction of the march is nearly in the prolongation of the line, and when a regiment arriving on the flank of a line already formed has to lengthen out that line.

S. 27. When the open Column changes its Front, and leading Flank, by the Countermarch of its Divisions, each on its own Ground.

DIVISIONS WILL COUNTERMARCH. { The column being halted, the pivot coverer takes exactly the place of his leader, but stands with his horse facing to the *rear*.

FROM THE ——
BY THE REAR FILE!
MARCH!
FORM —— DRESS! { The whole divisions then FILE from their reverse flanks, each by its own rear, and such flank (now to become its pivot one) is brought up, the front rank man to the stationed person.—The following files *close* in to their leaders, the column stands square, but facing to its former rear, and the coverer reins back to make place for the proper flank leader.—The column has thus changed its front and leading flanks.

In the countermarch, the filing is always from the flank which is not the pivot, but is to become such, and the conducting officers will lead out to a distance of half the front of their divisions before they begin to countermarch.

This countermarch of each division is an evolution of great utility.—It is equivalent to the WHEEL ABOUT of each division of the open column, but without altering the line of pivots, or their true covering.—It at once changes the front of a column. It enables a column marching in an alignement to return along the same line, and to take such new position in it as circumstances may require, without inverting the front of the line.— It applies to the half and quarter, as well as full and open column. In many situations of forming from column into line, it becomes a necessary previous operation.

When a column has thus countermarched by divifions, unlefs the divifions are equal, the diftances will not be the true wheeling up ones, but will be fuch as are equal to the front of the preceding divifion, and therefore the true diftances muft be regained before the divifions can truly wheel up into line.

S. 28. *When the open Column changes its leading Flank, by bringing up the rear Divifion to the Front, fucceffively followed by each other.*

Halt! Caution. *Three's right Wheel!* *March!* *Halt! Drefs!* *March!* *Halt!* *Wheel up!* *Halt! Drefs!* *March!*	If the right of the regiment is in front, the left to be brought up, and the column to continue to advance.—The whole is ordered to Halt!—At the caution Left Wing to the front, the leader of the left (the rear) divifion immediately orders it, *Three's right Wheel! March!* till his left flank can freely pafs the right flank of the others. He then commands *Halt! Wheel up! March!* clofe by the right flank of the divifion then preceding him, he himfelf being now on the right, which becomes his pivot flank.
Three's right Wheel! *March!* *Halt! Drefs!* *March!* *Halt!* *Wheel up!* *Halt! Drefs!* *March!*	The officer commanding his preceding divifion, as foon as the other approaches him, orders *Three's right Wheel! March!* behind the now leading one. *Halt! Wheel up!* when he covers, and then *March!* when at the due wheeling diftance. All the other divifions fucceffively perform the fame operation, and when

} when the right divifion has taken its place in the rear, the whole column is in perfect order, and proceeding in whatever direction is given to it.

If the column before this operation ftands clofed to half or quarter diftance, then each divifion proceeds as above directed, and takes its diftance from its preceding one, before it moves on.

S. 29. *Change of Front, by the Countermarch of the Squadron or Regiment.*

The *countermarch* changes the front and flanks of a body, and faces it to a rear, and is equivalent to a wheel of the half circle, made on any of its parts or points. It is *fucceffive*, (the body being halted) by each of its parts wheeling fucceffively on its own ground, as it comes to its turn. Or *progreffive*, (the body being in motion) by each part wheeling, when it comes up to the point at which the leading part wheeled, and begun the countermarch. In the firft cafe, the body muft fhift its ground a fpace at leaft equal to its front.

In the fecond, it will perform this operation of the countermarch on its original ground, exchanging flanks and front.

The *countermarch* from one flank to the other, may be made either before or behind the body. When from both flanks, it will be made both before and behind the body.—Markers will always be placed, to give the precife ground on which the countermarch is to be made. The column of countermarch muft at no rate improperly lengthen out, and the wheels of its parts muft be firm and rapid.

Squadron.

The squadron will countermarch from either flank—by file; ranks by two's, or ranks by three's, in the manner prescribed for the divisions of a column.

The squadron will countermarch from one flank by sub-divisions.—Sub-divisions will wheel to the flank.—The leading one will then wheel the half circle, and proceed along the flank of the squadron, by the sub-divisions of which it is followed, till the flanks have exchanged places.

The whole being then in column, wheel to their pivots into line.

The squadron will change front to the rear, by the wheels of half squadrons.—One half squadron advances a little more than its own length, and halts.—Both half squadrons wheel about inwards.—The retired half squadron moves up and joins the other.—A half squadron or division, or any small body, may change front in the same manner, by the wheels of its half parts.

The squadron changes front by wheeling on its center.—Half the squadron goes about ranks by three's.—The squadron wheels about on its standard.—The half squadron comes about by three's, and the squadron is fronted to its former rear.—Half squadrons or divisions may change front in the same manner.

Regiment.

The regiment may countermarch from one, or from both flanks; by the wheels of divisions, sub-divisions, ranks by three's or two's—and the squadrons of regiments will be mindful of the operation of their interval distances, by whatever kind of column they move—or it may countermarch on its center, or any other point by sub-divisions.—Or change front, each squadron by wheels of half squadron, or squadron, in the manner before directed.

S. 30. *Diminishing or increasing the Front of the Column of March.*

The column of march or manœuvre, in confequence of obftructions in its route, which it cannot furround, is frequently obliged to diminifh its front, and again to increafe it when fuch difficulties are paffed; it is one of the moft important of movements, and a regiment which does not perform this operation with the greateft exactnefs and attention, fo as not to lengthen out in the fmalleft degree, is not fit to move in the column of a confiderable corps.

The diminution or increafe of the front of the column, is performed by the fquadron when in movement, or when halted. In movement, this operation is either done by each divifion fucceffively, when it arrives at the point where the leading one of the column performed it; or elfe by the whole divifions of the fquadron at the fame moment. In either cafe, the chief of the fquadron, at the inftant that it fhould begin to reduce or increafe its front, gives the general CAUTION fo to do, and the leaders of divifions give their words of execution to the fub-divifions to double behind, or move up brifkly to the regulating ones, which preferve their original diftances from each other, and never alter the pace at which the column was marching, but proceed as if they were totally unconnected with the operation that the others are performing.

CLOSE COLUMN.

The great object of a confiderable clofe column is, to form the line to the front in the quickeft manner poffible; to conceal numbers from the knowledge of the adverfary; and to extend in whatever direction the circumftance of the cafe may require, which, till it is nearly accomplifhed, cannot be obvious to an oppofite enemy. It is a fituation for the affembly, more than for the movement of troops. It is not formed until the head of the

the troops is arrived in column, of whole, half, or quarter diftance, near the ground where they are to extend into line.

The formation from clofe column into line, is an original one; often protected by cannon, made at fuch a diftance, as not to fear interruption from an enemy; and avoiding the enfilade of artillery. Its pofitions cannot fail to be truly taken.

The clofe column may generally be compofed of half fquadrons, for the purpofe of movement. But when halted and to deploy, it may then double its front, and ftand in fquadrons.

In the clofe column, when ready to deploy into line, there is a diftance of two horfes' length between regiment and regiment—of one horfe's length between fquadrons of the regiment—of half a horfe's length between the divifions and ranks of fquadrons. Officers and their coverers, are on the pivot flanks of their divifions— colours and fupernumeraries are on the flanks, not the pivot ones; and mufic, farriers, or certain fupernumeraries, may alfo be in the rear of the regiment, no fingle perfons are between the ranks.

When the clofe column is formed and halted, the commanding officer (alone) gives orders for its MARCH! HALT! and commencement of formation in line.

A clofe column muft loofen its divifions before it can well march in front, and its changes of direction muft be made circling, and on a moving flank, to enable its rear gradually to comply. If too great intervals fhould be made in the column, they can beft be clofed by a halt of the head.

The clofe column is formed from line, or from the column of march.

When the regiment from line forms clofe column, it is neceffary to difengage the heads of its divifions from one another, that they may the fooner and eafier arrive at their pofition; this they do, *by wheeling to the hand ordered an eighth wheel* (of the quarter circle), they then

wheel

wheel ranks by threes to their leading flank, march to their place in column, and each wheels up by threes, which again forms the divifion.

S. 31. *The clofe Column may be formed from Line in front or rear of either of the Flank Half Squadrons, or in front or rear of any central one.*

If the Column is to ſtand faced as the Line is.

1. If in front of a flank divifion—the eighth wheel is outwards, or from that divifion, and three's break to their front leading flank.

2. If in rear of a flank divifion, the eighth wheel is inwards, or towards that divifion; and the three's break to their rear or leading hand.

3. If in front and rear of a central divifion—the eighth wheel is towards the hand which is to be the head of the column; viz. to the right, if the right is to be in front; and to the left, if the left is to be in front; and the three's break to their conducting hand.

If the Column is to ſtand faced to the Rear.

1. If in front of a flank divifion—that divifion is countermarched, the eighth wheel is made outwards, or from that divifion; and three's break to what was the ſtanding flank, or their rear hand.

2. If in rear of a flank divifion—that divifion is countermarched, the eighth wheel is inwards, or to that divifion; and three's break to the flank that wheeled up, or their front hand.

3. If in front and rear of a central divifion—that divifion is countermarched, the eighth wheel is towards the

the flank, which is to be the head of the column—and the divifions break by three's to their conducting hand.

On this occafion advantage will arife, if the *eighth wheel* is made on the center of each body, which does fo wheel; as it will more effectually difengage the leading flanks.

S. 32. *When the Regiment from Line forms clofe Column.*

1. *Before or behind either of the Flank Half Squadrons.*

CAUTION.	A CAUTION will exprefs the half fquadron, and whether the formation is in front or rear of it: and a new pofition may be given to it, and its leader fhifts, if neceffary, to that flank which is to become the pivot one of the column, and another perfon places himfelf ten or twenty yards before or behind him, according to circumftances, to mark the perpendicular and pivot line of the column.
HALF SQUADRONS TO THE—WHEEL! MARCH! HALT! DRESS!	The half fquadrons of the regiment will eight wheel (of the quarter circle) to the hand ordered.
THREE's--WHEEL! MARCH! *Halt, Drefs!*	The half fquadrons will WHEEL by three's, to which ever hand conducts them to their place in the clofe column, and leaders will fhift accordingly.
MARCH!	The whole will MARCH to the front or rear of the named half fquadron,

Halt! *Wheel up!* *Halt! Dress!*	squadron, and each leader will proceed in the same manner as in forming open column from line (except that pivot markers are not sent out) stopping in his own person at his pivot point, and giving his words to *halt*, *wheel up*, and *dress*, to his half squadron, when it has arrived upon the proper ground on which it is to stand in close column.
	During the formation of the close column, as soon as the regiment is put in motion, the commanding officer will immediately place himself before the officer of the directing half squadron, and see that the pivot leaders cover each other in the perpendicular direction, whether such covering is taken from before or behind.

2. *On a central Half Squadron.*

Caution.	A caution of formation is given. ——The named half squadron will stand fast, or be otherwise placed; its leader will place himself on its future pivot flank, and the line of pivots will be ascertained by a detached person.
—— Eighth Wheel! March! *Halt! Dress!* Three's —— Wheel! March! Halt! Dress!	The half squadrons of the regiment will wheel towards the hand which is to be in front of the column, and leaders will shift accordingly.

March!

March!	At the word MARCH! the reſt of the formation will proceed as before directed, part of the regiment arranging itſelf before and part behind the given half ſquadron, and the officers covering on the proper pivot flank.
Halt!	
Wheel up!	
Halt! Dreſs!	

In forming cloſe column facing to the rear, the ſame operations take place as to the front, with this difference, that the named half ſquadron countermarches; and the other half ſquadrons of the regiment wheel as directed, and lead from ſuch flanks as eſtabliſh a countermarch of the whole.

In the ſame manner in which cloſe columns are here formed from line, may *columns at half or quarter diſtance* alſo generally be formed, obſerving that in ſuch caſes, pivot flank points are given by markers, as in the formation in open column.

If the cloſe column of ſquadrons is formed from line.— The intervals between them prevent the neceſſity of their making the eight wheel:—they will, therefore, at once break by three's to their leading flank, and march to their places in column, as before directed.

S. 33. *When the Column marches to a Flank.*

Caution.	A CAUTION will expreſs to which flank. If to that which is not the pivot, the leading officer and coverer of each is ORDERED to move quickly by the rear of their diviſions to that flank, and the ſerrefiles and colours who were

	were on that flank, exchange to the other.
THREE'S TO THE ——WHEEL! MARCH! *Halt! Drefs!* MARCH!	The whole will WHEEL by three's to the flank, and be put in MARCH, the officer that leads the front divifion taking care to move in the exact alignement which is prolonged for him, and all the others, in preferving their proper fituations, drefs and move by him.
HALT! WHEEL UP! HALT! DRESS!	When the the column HALTS and WHEELS UP by three's, the pivot leaders are ORDERED to fhift to their proper places (if not already at them) by the rear of their divifions, unlefs the intended and immediate formation of the line, requires their remaining where they are.

S. 34. *When the Column marches to the Front.*

MARCH! CAUTION!	The whole advance at the word MARCH! If it is intended to loofen the column, a CAUTION fo to do will be given, the whole
HALT! *March!*	will HALT, except the leading divifion, and each divifion will again fucceffively *march* at a horfe's diftance.
HALT!	When the general word HALT! is given, the column halts as it is then placed; but if a partial and low word *Halt!* is given to the leading divifion only, the others move on ftill, and *halt* fucceffively

in

{ in close column, by word from their leaders.

S. 35. *When the Column is to change Direction.*

If halted.

CAUTION! { A CAUTION will be given that it is to change direction either to the right or left. The front division of the column is *wheeled* up into the new direction, and an advanced person is placed to determine the future line of pivots.

THREE's WHEEL! { The other divisions will WHEEL
MARCH! by three's to the ordered flank;
Halt! Dress! MARCH! *Halt! Wheel up!* and
MARCH! cover in column. If this move-
Halt! ment is made by the reverse flank,
Wheel up! no shifting of leaders will be re-
Halt! Dress! quired, but one of the serrefile officers already there, will conduct the flank movement of each, the words of command being still given by the proper pivot leader to *halt* and *wheel up*.

If in march.

If gradual and inconsiderable changes of direction are to be made during the march of the columns, the HEAD will, on a moveable pivot, effect such change, while all the other divisions, by advancing a shoulder, and inclining up to the flank which is the wheeling one, will successively conform to each other, and to the leading division, divifion, fo that at the word *forward*, they may move on in the ftraight line.

S. 36. *When the Column is to make Front to its Rear, by the Countermarch of its Divifions.*

THE COLUMN WILL COUNTERMARCH!	If the divifions are at a fufficient distance to allow of it, they will each feparately, on its own ground, countermarch, as directed for open column.
EVEN DIVISIONS, RIGHT FILE! MARCH! *Form!*	If the column is quite clofe, the whole will prepare to *file* from the reverfe flank. The even, or every other divifion (reckoning from the head) will *file* to the flank, and form, fo that their pivot flank may be three or four paces clear of the column.
THE WHOLE WILL COUNTERMARCH! MARCH! *Halt! Form! Drefs!*	They are then ordered to COUNTERMARCH towards the column, and at the fame word, the odd divifions, which have hitherto ftood ftill, countermarch alfo, each on its own ground; the even divifions *file* on till they are again in their proper places in column, and *halt, form*.

DEPLOYMENT INTO LINE.

The clofe column of the regiment forms in line on its front, or its rear, or on any central divifion, by the DEPLOYMENT or flank march by three's, and by which it fucceffively uncovers and extends its feveral divifions.

Before the clofe column deploys, its head divifion, whether it is halted or in movement, muft be on the line into which it is to extend. That line is therefore the prolongation of the head divifion, and fuch points in it, to one or both flanks, as are neceffary for the formation of the regiment, are immediately taken.

The flank march muft be made quick, parallel to the general line, and without opening out, the moft particular precifion is therefore required. Each divifion, when oppofite to its ground in line, will be moft advantageoufly halted, and wheeled up (or at leaft corrected) by a detached field officer of the regiment; in cafe its leader fhould not be critical in his commands, or, that he fhould not be heard; or, that his three's are too open; and thus may the defects of a preceding divifion be remedied, by the judicious ftop of the one following it. The divifion is then brought up into line by its refpective leader. The juftnefs of formations depends altogether on officers judging their diftances, and timing their commands.

The officer, in leading his divifion into line, muft bring it up perfectly fquare. His dreffing is always from the laft come up divifion, towards the other flank, and the eyes of all are turned to that divifion, and the formed part of the line.

As the head of the clofe column is always brought up to the line on which it is to extend, therefore, when the formation is made on the rear, or on a central divifion, fuch divifion, when uncovered, muft move up to the identical ground which the front has quitted.

S. 37. *When the Regiment in clofe Column of Half Squadrons,* (fuppofe the Right in Front) *deploys into Line.*

1. *On the front Divifion.*

The column being halted with its front divifion in the alignement

| | ment, and all the others in their true situations, parallel, and well closed up to it, a point of forming and dressing upon is taken, in the prolongation of that division (before the flanks of which two markers are placed) and towards where the left of the regiment is
CAUTION. | to extend. A CAUTION is given that the line will form on the front division.

THREE'S LEFT WHEEL! MARCH! *Halt! Dress!*
  At the words, THREE'S LEFT WHEEL! MARCH! *Halt! Dress!* the front division stands fast, its leader shifting to the right, and all the others wheel, (in this case always to the pivot flank).

MARCH!
  At the word MARCH! they go off quick, with heads dressed, moving parallel (not oblique) to the line of formation, the three's close and compact, so as not to open the divisions out.

Halt!
Wheel up!
Halt! Dress!
March!
  The leader of the second or leading division having moved out to his right, at the above word, march, allows his division, led by his coverer, to go on a space equal to its front (serrefiles exclusive) and then gives his words, *Halt! Wheel up! Halt, Dress!* and corrects and squares his division, then brings it to the alignement, giving the words, *March! Halt, Dress!* leaving the accurate dressing to the squadron officer, who is on the right flank (of squadron) for that purpose.

Halt! Dress!
  In this manner every other division proceeds, each being successively

{ ceffively fronted, marched up, and halted.

The divifions, which give the intervals of fquadrons, muft take care to front oppofite their ground in line, and fend up a marker to give the interval flank. The ftandard will come up in its place with the right half fquadron. The ferrefiles will halt when their divifions front; and when the movement of the other divifions allow of it, they will place themfelves behind their own proper ones.

---

2. *On the Rear Divifion.*

The column being placed as before directed, and a point of forming taken to the right in the prolongation of the head divifion, and towards where the right of the regiment is to come.

CAUTION.

A CAUTION is given, that the line will be formed on the rear divifion. The leaders of divifions, and their coverers (except thofe of the rear divifion) will immediately be ORDERED to pafs behind their feveral divifions, and poft themfelves on the right of each, exchanging places with their ferrefiles.

Two under officers are fent from the rear divifion, to place themfelves exactly before the flank files of the front divifion, and the leader of the front divifion is fhewn the point in the alignement on which he is to march, taking his intermediate points if neceffary.

The

THREE's RIGHT WHEEL! MARCH! *Halt! Drefs!*	The words, THREE's RIGHT WHEEL! MARCH! *Halt, Drefs!* are then given, and all the divifions, except the rear one, wheel threes to the right (in this cafe always to the reverfe flank.)
MARCH!	At the word MARCH! the wheeled divifions move on quick; their heads are dreffed to the left; the front one moves in the alignement, and the others parallel, and clofe on its right.
March! *Halt! Drefs!*	As foon as the rear divifion is uncovered, it receives the word, *March!* and proceeds. When within a few yards of its ground, its leader moves brifkly up to the marker of its left in the new pofition, and there in due time gives his words, *Halt, Drefs!* quickly correcting his divifion on the diftant point of formation.
Halt! *Wheel up!* *Halt! Drefs!* *March!*	In the mean time the leader of the divifion which immediately precedes the rear one, having at the firft word MARCH! gone brifkly round to the rear of his divifion, without impeding its movement, and having allowed it to move on, led by his coverer, gives his words to *Halt! Wheel up! Halt, Drefs!* when his divifion has marched a diftance equal to its front, and thereby uncovered the one behind it (which as already mentioned, immediately moves forward) he then places himfelf on its left. As foon as his own front is clear, he gives his word, *March!* his divifion proceeds to the alignement, where

Halt, Drefs!	where he gives his words *Halt, Drefs!* when his own left joins the right of the half fquadron formed on. The fquadron officers dreffing and correcting as in the preceding deployment. The markers of intervals, ftandard, and ferrefiles, proceed as already mentioned.
Halt! Wheel up! *Halt, Drefs!*	All the other divifions fuccefſively are conducted in the fame manner, until the right one (which has been marching critically in the alignement, and on no account getting before it) receives, when it arrives on its juft ground, the words to *Halt! Wheel up!* and *Drefs!*

3. *On a Central Divifion.*

Forming points muſt be given to both flanks in the prolongation of the head divifion. At the CAUTION of forming on a central divifion, the leading officers, and ferrefiles, will ſhift accordingly. The divifions in front of the named one wheel to one flank; thoſe in the rear of it to the other; according to the hand which leads to their ground. The named divifion, when uncovered, moves up into line to its marked flank; thoſe that were in front of it proceed as in forming on a rear divifion; thoſe that are in the rear of it, proceed as in forming on a front divifion.

S. 38. *Oblique Deployment of the cloſe Column into Line.*

1. *On an oblique Line advanced.*

The front divifion is wheeled up into a new direction on its *reverſe* flank, and the line is prolonged.

The

The divisions of the column are wheeled up to the hand
it deploys to. The leaders of divisions then turn their
horses so as themselves to take a direction parallel to the
given one. The whole are put in march, and the rear
of the divisions gradually get into the square direction of
their heads, which proceed and form as usual.

In this movement the heads of the divisions will be a
little retired behind each other, the rear leaders will take
great care not to close on each other, nor the head which
conducts them. Much precision is also required in justly timing the *Halt, Wheel up!* of each division, which
by that time ought to be moving perfectly parallel to the
line of formation.

2. *On an oblique Line retired.*

The front division is wheeled upon its pivot flank
into the new direction, and the line is prolonged. The
same operation, though more difficult, takes place, as
when the line is advanced, and the rear divisions must
take particular care to ease from and yield to the march
of the front. The head division being advanced a few
paces before it takes the oblique direction, will give a
facility to the heads of the rear divisions in gradually
gaining it.

Such deployment can hardly be required on any other
than the front division of the close column. Particular
attention is necessary, to give every aid as to the points
of forming, and to the heads of divisions moving as soon
as possible parallel to and behind the line.

S. 39. *When the close Column halted is to
form in Line in the Prolongation of its
Flanks, and on a front, or rear, or central
Division.*

{ The caution of formation is
given. The named division stands
fast.

MARCH!	faft, the others march forward in clofe column in the given line. Their pivot officers fucceflively take wheeling diftance from each other, beginning at the named one, and fucceflively give their word
Halt!	halt! as each has acquired it. When the whole is in open column, the line is formed by a wheel up to a flank. In this manner diftances are begun to be taken from the rear. But when
THREE'S ABOUT! MARCH! HALT, DRESS! MARCH! Halt! Front! Halt! Drefs!	the named divifion is a front or central one, the others that are behind it muft wheel three's about, MARCH forward, take their diftances, and FRONT fucceflively.

The column may alfo be opened from any named divifion, by the leading one only marching off and each other fucceflively following, as wheeling diftance is acquired from the one preceding. When the whole have opened, the general word HALT! is given, or the column is allowed to proceed.

S. 40. When the Column clofed to half diftance forms in Line to its Front on any Divifion.

The line will be formed either by the deployments of the clofe column, or by the flank marches of the divifions of the open column, and there wheel up into line; or by a fharp incline of divifions into line. In every cafe, care muft be taken to have a fufficiency of points eftablifhed to enfure the true direction of the line.

From column at quarter diftance the line may be formed to any front, and on any divifion, by the movements of the clofe and open column.

CHANGES

CHANGES OF POSITION OF THE REGIMENT BY THE ECHELLON (or diagonal) MOVEMENT.

The echellon position and movements are not only necessary and applicable to the immediate attacks and retreats of great bodies, but also to the previous *oblique* or direct changes of situation, which a regiment or corps formed in line, may be obliged to make to its front or rear, or on a particular fixed division of the line. Echellon of march in changes of position.

The oblique changes are produced by the wheel less than the quarter circle, of divisions from line, which places them in the echellon situation, ready to move. The *direct* changes are produced by the perpendicular and successive march of divisions from line, to front or rear. How formed.

The march in the direct echellon produces new parallel positions to front or rear. The march in echellon when formed by the wheels of the divisions from line, produces new oblique positions to front or rear, and at the same time to the flank, according to the degree of wheel given to the echellon. How applied.

The march in open column produces new prolonged positions to either flank.

The echellon of march necessary in making changes of situation, will be composed of half-squadrons or divisions, and formed from line by the wheel of each forward on its own flank, to the hand to which it is to move, and such wheel must be less than the quarter circle, for in such case the body would be in open column.

To form the echellon of oblique march, the degree of wheel made up from line ought strictly to be such as will place the divisions perpendicular to their future points of march; but in practice generally, the *half*, *quarter*, or *eighth wheel* (of the quarter circle) each ordered according to circumstances, may suffice to attain the proper end. Degree of wheel into echellon.

The echellon may be considered as a column of a particular kind, as well as the open column; they are easily
converted

converted into each other, by a new degree of wheel of each of their component divifions.

S. 41. *When from Line, the Half-fquadrons of a Regiment march off in Echellon fucceffively and directly forward to the Front and again form in Line, either to the Front or to the Flank.*

1. *As long as the intention is to form again to that front*—They may be retired at any *named* diftance behind each other, and when the leading divifion *halts,* the others may move on, and drefs in line with it.

2. *But when the intention is to form in line to the flank*—The whole will be ordered to HALT, or the divifions to take any named diftance and *halt.* The directing flank of the leading divifion will be confidered as the firft point in the intended oblique line, and the particular direction meant to be given it, will be eftablifhed by the placing of another point beyond and before it. A marker from each divifion will quickly move out, and place themfelves as pivots, lining on the firft given points, and on each other; each alfo taking a diftance from the one before him, equal to the front of the divifion which precedes him.

The rear divifions are then, by inclining to their directing hands, or by flank marching, moving up, and fhoulders forward, MARCHED to their refpective markers, and halted on the line. Or the divifions, inftead of forming in line, may be ordered to HALT in echellon at their feveral markers, and parallel to their former front. The whole is then put in march forward, and preferving their relative fituations, HALT, and WHEEL BACK into line, at fome more advanced point.

S. 42. *When a Regiment from Line wheels forward by Half Squadrons or Divisions to either Flank, into oblique Echellon, and Halts.*

CAUTION.

DIVISIONS WILL MAKE AN EIGHT WHEEL TO——!

At the general CAUTION—That the divisions will wheel forward, so as to place them perpendicular to their future lines of march; a person from the leading division of each squadron marks the wheeling flank of that division, according to the degree ordered, whether *half*, *quarter*, or *eighth wheel*.

MARCH!
HALT! DRESS!

At the word MARCH! each division wheels up, and they receive the words HALT, DRESS! to the standing flank, to which the leaders of divisions (as necessary) have shifted.

When the movement is to be the rear instead of the front—the regiment will wheel about by three's; wheel forward into echellon, in the above manner; and proceed as if the line was to its proper front.

S. 43. *When a Regiment or Line is to change its Position on a fixed Flank, by throwing the other Flank forward or backward, and by the Echellon march of Divisions.*

1. *When a Flank is thrown forward.*

The new direction is ascertained by two persons, placed beyond the flank, and the flank division is accurately wheeled into it.

DIVISIONS— WHEEL! MARCH! HALT! DRESS!	The other fimilar divifions of the line are (each upon its inward flank) wheeled up *half* as much as the flank divifion wheeled, and thus ftand in echellon, the pivot leaders placing themfelves on the inward flank.
MARCH!	The whole, except the flank divifion, are then put in MARCH, each looking to its leader, who is on its inward flank, and thus advancing perpendicularly towards its point in the new line.

Before the leading divifion of each fquadron has reached the line, a marker will move forward quickly to prolong it, and place himfelf rather beyond where his rear divifion is to come up; fo that there fhall be always at leaft one fixed object to correct upon beyond each divifion, as it halts in line.

Shoulders forward! *Forward!* *Halt, Drefs!*	When the officer, conducting the fecond divifion, arrives within twenty or twenty-five paces of where he is to join the firft divifion already placed, he gives a word, *Shoulder* (the outward one) *forward!* on which the man next to himfelf gradually turns his horfe, fo as to arrive in the new line, perfectly fquare in his own perfon; and the reft of his divifion (who till this inftant have marched in their original perpendicular direction) conforming to him, and proportionally quickening their pace, arrive in full parallel front on the line, fo as to have a very fmall movement to make at the words *Halt! Drefs!* which is given when his leading flank touches the flank of his preceding divifion; and inftantly refumes

| | fumes his place in fquadron, leaving the correct dreffing to the fquadron officer. |

	In this manner divifion will come up after divifion, each following one obferving to give the word *Shoulders forward!* when the preceding one gets the words *Halt! Drefs!* and each, after bringing up his divifion, fhifts to his poft in fquadron.
Shoulders forward! *Forward!* *Halt! Drefs!*	

The exact formation in this oblique line depends totally on the divifions having wheeled (only) one half of the angle, which the new pofition makes with the old one; for fhould they at firft wheel up the whole of that angle, they would then be marching parallel to that line, and arrive in it doubled behind each other; whereas, by having the other half of the wheel to complete when they come near to the new pofition, each moves in a perpendicular direction, and difengages the ground required by the fucceeding one to form upon.

---

2. *When a Flank is thrown backward.*

The direction is afcertained as before, and the flank divifion *placed* on it.

THREE'S ABOUT! MARCH! HALT! DRESS!	The fquadrons of the line go *about* ranks by three's.
DIVISIONS— WHEEL! MARCH! HALT! DRESS!	The divifions of fquadrons make their *ordered degree* of wheel towards the placed divifion.
MARCH!	The divifions MARCH with the rear ranks in front, and form in line, in the fame manner as when changing pofition forward; except

—*Shoulder forward!* *Forward!*	cept that the leader of each, when he arrives within twenty or twenty-five paces of the line, will give his word, *Shoulder forward!* and thereby gradually bring up his division to be parallel to the line; he himself having ftopt at the line, will, as foon as his flank front rank man comes to the preceding formed rear rank man, give his words to *Halt! Front! Halt! Drefs! March! Halt! Drefs!* in the general line on the point which is prepared for him beyond the flank of his own fquadron.
Halt, front! *Halt! Drefs!* *March!* *Halt! Drefs!*	

Very great activity is required from the leader in drefsing up, or drefsing back of his divifion, otherwife the point of appui (viz. his own fartheft flank) will not be ready for the next leader, who is to arrive at and begin from it to perform the fame operation, and this will particularly happen where the change of direction is inconfiderable.

In the fuccefsive drefsing up or back of divifions, officers are to be careful always to line them, fo as not to obfcure the marking perfons, but to leave them open and diftinct, fo that the direction of the line may run horfe's head to horfe's head of the markers.

---

3. *When the Change is on a Central Divifion, one Flank being thrown forward, and the other backward.*

The direction of the new line is afcertained, and the central divifion placed on it.

THREE'S ABOUT! *March!* *Halt! Drefs!*	The fquadrons of the retiring wing go ABOUT by three's.

DIVI-

DIVISIONS- RIGHT WHEEL! MARCH! HALT, DRESS!
: The divisions of the squadrons of each wing make the *ordered degree* of wheel inwards and forwards, so as to face to the placed division.

MARCH!
: The whole MARCH forward into line with the central division, the advancing wing dressing up, and the retiring wing again fronting and dressing in line; as already described.

S. 44. *March in Line.*

The march of the line in front is the most difficult, and the most material of all movements; it is requisite near the enemy, and immediately precedes the attack. In proportion to the extent of front, and rapidity required, does that difficulty encrease; therefore too much exactness and minuteness in the execution of it cannot be observed.

March in line.

When marching in line, each squadron dresses to its own center, which center follows its own leader, the several leaders line with, and preserve distances from each other, and from the regulating squadron; this alone has its objects of march, the others being all subordinate to, and conforming to its motions.

General Attention.

When parts of a line marching in front are interrupted by any obstacle, they must halt, and by flank movements of their divisions or subdivisions, double behind (into close column) such adjoining parts as are not so interrupted, and avoid pressing upon them. In proportion as they pass such obstacle, and that the ground permits them to come into line, they will in the same manner, by flank movements, move up into their proper places, where a void space has been preserved for them. If only small portions of a line are interrupted, and for a short space, they may follow in file, or rather in ranks,

Passing obstacles.

Column.

by

by three's or two's behind the flanks of the uninterrupted parts, and move up to their places in file (or by three's or two's) when it can be done.

Halt of the line.
When the line halts, each fquadron halts and dreffes by its own center; and if the dreffing of the general line is to be afterwards corrected, it ought to begin at, and be taken from the regulating fquadron.

Succeffive halt of fquadrons.
The line fhould always be in fo correct a fituation, as to halt inftantly at the word, *Halt!* but if at any time the difficulties of ground have unavoidably thrown fquadrons out of the line, in fuch cafe, the halt of thofe fquadrons will be fucceffive as they regain their proper fituations.

Standards.
The ftandards muft be always carried uniformly and upright, in order to facilitate the moving and dreffing of the line.

Dreffing the line after halting.
After the march and halt in line of each fquadron by its own center, if a more exact dreffing is required, then two perfons are placed with their horfes heads before the flank files of the regulating fquadron, which is previoufly dreft in the true direction; each other fquadron, from each flank, advances (directly forward) a perfon to prolong that line; all eyes are directed to the regulating fquadron; the whole (by fquadrons, either together or fucceffively, and quickly as ordered), move up and halt in the given line. A ftraight line is in this manner obtained; but if the intervals are falfe, they muft remain fo till corrected, by order, and by a feparate operation of flank marching.

Flank fquadron.
A flank-fquadron of a line need never remain an inftant with a falfe interval, or ill dreffed, as its corrections do not interfere with any part of the line.

S. 45. *When the Line advances.*

A line that is to advance, muft be before hand accurately formed and dreffed, to enable it to move in a direction perpendicular to its front, otherwife a floating,

open-

opening out, or closing in of its parts, will take place, till such perpendicular march is attained.

THE LINE WILL ADVANCE!
{ THE LINE WILL ADVANCE (by a named squadron), is a caution. The officer commanding such squadron, quickly determines by his eye the exact perpendicular to the front of the line which he is to march upon, and till he is satisfied the direction of it is just, he is not to look out for objects in it. Every other squadron remains prepared.

Any person, who means to indicate the direction of a line which is to be pursued (and the prolongation of which is not upon some strong object) to another person, will do it in the most ready manner, by himself riding some small distance forward in the intended direction, and desiring the person who has remained at a given point to take such line over his head, and of course to mark his points of marching in it.

MARCH!
{ At the word MARCH! instantly repeated to each squadron, the whole move; each squadron by its center, and each squadron leader attentive to, and preserving his pace, line, and distance, from his directing hand. If the whole move uniformly and straight forward, the line will be firm and steady. If any inaccuracy arises, it must be instantly remedied by the inclining, moving up, or keeping back of particular squadrons, and such necessary alterations must be made, by firm command and judicious execution, so as not to affect the general line. The attention of commanding officers is extended to the general line, and they are to avoid partaking of errors of any portion

	portion of it, that is evidently in the wrong; but, on the contrary, to confider fuch part as if deranged by fome occafional obftacle, and to preferve their own juft relative pofition with refpect to the directing fquadron.
HALT!	*If the line marches juft*, it will halt juftly, the whole at the fame inftant of the command HALT! If this is not the cafe, the halt of fquadrons muft be to a degree fucceffive; at any rate the fquadrons muft halt in the general line.

All alterations of pace muft be made in a firm and decided manner, and by the whole at the fame inftant, in confequence of the order repeated by fquadron leaders.

S. 46. *When the Line retires.*

THE neceffity of its being previoufly and correctly dreffed, is full as effential as when it is to advance; if that preliminary is not taken care of, its movements will be difordered in proportion to its extent.

THE LINE WILL RETIRE!	THE LINE WILL RETIRE, is a Caution—on which preparation is made in the fame manner as on advancing; the officer who leads the directing fquadron, immediately afcertains his point of march, and each fquadron has an officer (not the commanding one) placed behind its center, ready to lead to the rear.
THREE'S ABOUT! MARCH! HALT! DRESS!	RANKS BY THREE'S ABOUT— MARCH! on which the ranks and ferrefiles wheel about, and the fquadrons remain ready for the general word.

MARCH!

MARCH!	MARCH!—The line retires in the fame manner as it advances, and the commanding officers of fquadrons, being in the rear of the ftandards (each of his own) can by their eye and directions, give occafional aid.
HALT! FRONT! HALT! DRESS!	HALT—is the paufe of a moment. RANKS—by three's about. HALT! DRESS! by the ftandards.

If any further dreffing of the line is neceffary, it is ordered by the commander as already directed.

The line is never to remain halted an inftant after facing to the rear, but is immediately to march on. And when it halts, it is immediately to FRONT, and then to DRESS.

When the line is marching to the front or rear, the partial obftacles that prefent themfelves, will be paffed by the formation, march, and deployment of the clofe column. Such parts as are not interrupted ftill move on in front; fuch parts as are interrupted double by divifions as ordered behind an adjoining flank, or flanks, and in this manner follow in clofe column in their natural order. As the ground opens they fucceffively deploy, and again perfect the line. The columns are always behind the line, and march clofed up. The formed part of the regiments, whether advancing or retiring, continues to move on at the ordinary pace, and in proportion as the obftacles increafe or diminifh, will the formed, or column, parts of the line increafe or diminifh.

S. 47. *Retreat of the Regiment by alternate Half Squadrons.*

The regiment is told off by alternate, right and left, half fquadrons, and one of direction for each is announced.

One divifion of the regiment (the left) is ordered to ftand faft, the rights go three's about.

The retiring part marches a given diftance, and when ordered, halts and fronts; this ferves for a fignal to the advanced part of the regiment to begin its retreat in the fame manner, each body through its proper interval; and, when ordered, to halt and front. The alternate retreat is thus continued either at a walk or at a trot, till the line has attained fome new fituation, being covered by fuch fkirmifhers or light troops, as were originally advanced in the front for that purpofe, and who gradually fall back in proportion as the lines do.

Inverfion of the Line.

The fquadrons may be obliged to wheel by ranks or divifions to the right about, the more readily to oppofe a danger, inftead of changing a pofition by a countermarch. It may be under the neceffity of forming to a flank, its rear rank in front. The column with its right in front may arrive on the left of its ground, and be obliged immediately to form up, and fupport that point. But on the whole, it is to be recollected, that though the inverfion of fquadrons in a regiment ought to occafion no real inconvenience, yet that of the divifions of the fquadron within itfelf, would lead to diforder, and muft be ftudioufly avoided.

S. 48. *When without the help of advanced Objects, the Commander of a Line changes the pofition of the whole, or Part of it, to a Flank.*

In original formations of the line from column of march, preparatory points can always be given; *but, in changes of the line*, or *parts of it*, from one pofition to another, more advantageous with refpect to the enemy, and to making the attack, the new one muft often depend

pend on, and be taken up by, the eye of the commander only, while the whole is in motion, and who will himself conduct the movement.

The change being determined on, the movement being necessarily a quick one, and the body that is to make it being apprized accordingly, the commander places himself at the flank which is to lead, and has five or six detached persons with him, ready to take his orders.

The line breaks into column to the flank, (of divisions, sub-divisions, or ranks by three's, according as the ground allows; for in such an operation the column must be on such a front as it can maintain, till it again forms in line); on this occasion, the pivots being lined, and the wheeling distances being true, is most essential, and therefore if the divisions can form column backwards, it should be done.

The commander being before the pivot of the leading division puts the whole in motion, and conducts the head of the column, in such manner as he finds proper, towards the ground on which he proposes to form a new line, and to the pace and path of which head, the rest of the column must strictly conform.

When he arrives near to where he proposes his formation, with a glance of the eye, without stopping, and according to the enemy's situation, he determines the direction he is to give his line, and the point where he means to enter it, conducting his leading division, so as by a circling movement of the *shoulder forward,* to arrive with its pivot flank on the line on that point, he there halts a person to indicate the point of entry, (with his horse's head to the flank of the column) and pursues the direction, which is only known to himself, and in which he will always find and take intermediate points. From distance to distance he leaves persons placed in the above manner in the line, for the direction of the column pivots, which they are to take care successively to pass close to. He HALTS the column when he finds necessary. *Wheels* up into line—Is ready TO ADVANCE—And, ATTACK, in line or echellon.

S. 49. *Paſſage of Lines.*

If ſquadrons are to paſs through infantry in their front. When the line arrives cloſe behind them, each ſquadron will march from its center ranks by two's (eight men in front). They will all paſs at the ſame inſtant through the openings which are made for them, and at the diſtance of thirty yards the heads will halt and dreſs, the ſquadrons will form, and the line move on.

If the line has attacked and broken the enemy, and that ſmaller detachments than ſquadrons are to purſue, they will at the ordered inſtant march from a flank, ranks by two's, paſs the infantry, form up while in motion, and purſue with vigour.

A line of cavalry obliged to retire through a line of infantry, will, when arrived cloſe to the infantry, front, and inſtantly march off each half ſquadron (from its right flank) ranks by two's, ſtraight to the rear, wherever the heads of half-ſquadrons preſent themſelves, the infantry will make opening ſufficient for four horſes to paſs through. The heads of the half-ſquadrons remain dreſſed, and preſerve diſtances from the left. When at a ſufficient diſtance (in the rear) the open column is formed (right in front) by the cloſing in and wheeling up of the two's. Pivots being then adjuſted, the parallel line is formed by the wheeling up of the half-ſquadrons.

S. 50. *Attack of Cavalry in Front and Flank.*

The covering a flank in a line of cavalry, or having a body behind a flank, ready to turn that of the enemy, is of the greateſt conſequence, and their previous ſituation ſhould be concealed as much as poſſible. That flank which is not to be employed in turning the enemy, cannot be ſo well ſecured as by two or three half-ſquadrons

drons placed in echellon to the firſt line, about fifty paces from each other. With difficulty the enemy can turn this echellon, and it enables the other flank to act with more freedom. Theſe half-ſquadrons in echellon are kept refuſed or brought up into line according to circumſtances.

But behind the flank deſtined to turn that of the enemy, ſeveral half-ſquadrons may be placed at quarter-diſtance; at the ordered moment, the diviſions of the column will wheel to the flank ranks by three's; the head of the leading diviſion will take a new direction of the ſame degree at which an incline is made; to this all the reſt will, as ſoon as poſſible, conform; and when they have opened about one hundred yards from the line, the leading half-ſquadron will front, and move on a point taken fifty yards from the enemy's flank; the others continue their march rapidly by the flank, and paſſing each other, they ſucceſſively front and move on beyond each other, the whole being thus at firſt in an echellon to the rear, but which gradually changes to an echellon to the front, and at the finiſhing of the attack, the enemy's flank and rear is gained.

When flankers, ſkirmiſhers, or purſuers, are ordered out from the body of the ſquadron, they may in general be taken from one or both flank diviſions, and conſiſt of one or two complete ſub-diviſions, or one or two complete three's, thereby leaving every other part of the ſquadron entire; they will be commanded by appointed officers, move out at the inſtant of command, and proceed to perform thoſe duties in which every cavalry ſoldier of every kind muſt be individually inſtructed and practiſed, and be maſter of the uſe of his fire-arms and ſword, when ſingle, as well as in rank.

In a charge of either infantry or cavalry, though a momentary diſorder may take place, yet the inſtant the enemy gives way, the line muſt be again formed, and the purſuit continued by light troops, or by detached troops or companies only. Theſe follow the enemy with the utmoſt vigour, and as ſoon as the line is in order, it advances again and completes the defeat.

When cavalry attack infantry, they are apt to break, but it ought always to be remembered, that when the enemy is difperfed, they give up the purfuit to the fecond line, which is fupported by the firft as foon as it regains its order. Light cavalry are in general placed in the fecond line.

When cavalry attack cavalry, the fquadrons muft be firm and compact; but when they attack infantry, the files may be opened, and the men may bend down on their horfe's necks.

When cavalry attack infantry, they fhould in general do it in column; and the fquadrons of the column fhould have at leaft three times as much diftance between them as the extent of their front. The leading fquadron after breaking the enemy's line, fhould move forward and form; the two fucceeding ones fhould each wheel outwards by half fquadrons, and charge along the line; whatever other fquadrons follow will fupport and act according to circumftances.

It may be expected, that under a fevere fire both the cavalry and infantry lofe to a degree their regular order, before they arrive on the enemy; but cavalry acting againft cavalry, can profit by its manoeuvre and order till the very laft moment; for, till the horfes heads come up againft each other, there is nothing that ought to prevent a cavalry foldier from being as fteady in the ranks, as if he was at a common exercife.

S. 51. *The Column of Route or March.*

The column of march is the foundation of all diftant movements, and even of evolutions and manoeuvres.— It is in that manner that the columns of an army fhould perform their marches, that an enemy fhould be approached, and that fafety can be infured to the troops in their tranfitions from one point to another.

All marches, for any confiderable diftance, will at all times

times be made preferably, where the ground allows, in column of divisions of the line, viz. by half squadrons, or divisions, or sub-divisions, when the squadrons exceed forty files.——But where the breadth of the routes so require it, the march will be made by ranks by three's or two's; or finally, by the filing of ranks; this last is never to be done but in cases of absolute necessity.

What front made on.

All diminishing or increasing the front of a column of march, is in general done by each body of the column, at the point where the leading division first does it; such operation should be performed with quickness and firmness, so as if possible not thereby to retard or open out the column.—At all points of increasing or diminishing the front of the march, an intelligent officer should be stationed to see that it is performed with celerity; and the commander of a considerable column should have constant reports and inspections made, that the column is moving with proper regularity: he should have officers in advance to apprise him of difficulties to be avoided, or obstacles to be passed; and should himself apply every proper means to obviate such as may occur in the march.—The great principle, on all occasions, of diminishing or increasing the front of the column in march is, that such part as doubles, or forms up, shall slacken, or quicken its pace, as may be necessary to conform to the part which has no such operation to perform, but which continues its uniform march without the least alteration, as if no such process was going on; and if this is observed, distances can never be lost, or the column lengthened out.

Diminishing or increasing the front of the column.

Where a march is made near the enemy, if to a flank, the object must be, that at no time, if possible, the extent in column may be greater than the extent required in line; if to the front, or to the rear, then the object will be to march on a front of divisions, or half squadrons, with their distances closed up one half or more, that they may the more quickly deploy into a line when required; therefore, in such situations, if a column is obliged to diminish its front, from any obstacle in the route, it will, in general, after passing it, be ordered again to increase it,

March of the column near an enemy.

it, that it may be the better prepared for the great object of the march.

Attention of officers on the march.

On a march, there are so many occasional and temporary halts, that individual soldiers should at no other time be allowed to stop or dismount.—And when any of them are so permitted, it must be then evident, that the unavoidable halt will allow of this being done without affecting the march of the column.

No man must be permitted to ride in a careless lounging manner, which tends to fatigue and ruin the horse.—No one is to stop under pretence of watering his horse, much less is any division of the column to do so.—At a general halt, every necessary examination and adjustment of saddles, girths, &c. should be made.

Attention of commanding officers in column of march.

Regiments are not solely to depend on the one immediately before them for alteration of pace, or for the diminution or increase of the front of the column.—If there is reason to think that it has not originated from the front, they are to stop the mistake, and not continue it.——The look out of each commanding officer must be as forward as possible, at the same time that he is to recollect, in the execution of any of the operations of the column, how he can aid in moderating the difficulties and fatigue that always go on increasing to those behind him.

Change of direction.

The necessary changes in the direction of the route are gradually made by the divisions of the column, as on a moveable pivot, and not by quick and square wheels, unless the divisions are confined on each flank, and thereby obliged to make fixed wheels to prevent the loss of intervals.

Baggage.

On a march, servants, led horses, and canteen horses, remain with their squadrons.—The situation and movements of carriages belonging to the column, is prescribed in orders.

The place of the bat-horses is always ascertained for them, in the order in which their regiments follow each other: they are never to march in the divisions of the troops,

troops, but in front or rear of the whole column, according to circumftances, and as fhall be directed: a fufficient guard is to be with thofe of each regiment, and great care taken that they do not fall behind, ftraggle, or extend the column.

It is feldom that the bat-horfes can be ordered to march on the flank of the column; it ought only to be in ground where there is a certainty that no defile can occur, for in fuch cafe, they cannot be permitted to enter into the column, but muft ftop till the troops have paffed, and follow in rear.—When they do move on a flank, it is always on that flank which is not next the enemy.

EVOLUTIONS.

DIVISIONS, FROM THE RIGHT MARCH IN COLUMN TO THE FRONT. } A Caution.

DIVISIONS!
  RIGHT WHEEL!
  MARCH!
  HALT, DRESS!
  MARCH!
  HALT!

The divisions are wheeled to the right, except the first, which moves forward at the word march! to the left flank of the second division, and is there halted by its officer, who has shifted during the wheel (by the rear) for that purpose; at the word march, the whole move forward as far as necessary, and are there halted.*

FORM SQUADRON ON THE FRONT DIVISION BY THE OBLIQUE MARCH! } A Caution.

DIVISIONS, RIGHT BACK, HALF WHEEL!
  MARCH!
  Halt, Dress!
  MARCH!
  Left shoulder forward!
  Forward!
  Halt! Dress!

At this caution, the officers shift by the front, to the right of their divisions, and *halt, dress,* when the half wheel is completed: at the word MARCH! they conduct them into line, giving the word, *left shoulder forward!* in proper time, so as to enable them to gain the half wheel required.

COLUMNS OF DIVISIONS, FROM THE LEFT MOVE OFF TO THE REAR! } A Caution.

---

* If the squadron consists of 48 files, or upwards, the movement both to front and rear may be made by sub-divisions.

Divisions, left wheel! March! Halt, Dress! March! *Left Wheel!* *Halt, Dress!* *March!*	The divisions *wheel* to the left, and at the second word, March! the leading one again wheels to the left. The other divisions move on, and again separately wheel to the left as they cover and follow in open column the leading division, which advances at such pace as is ordered.
On the leading division, to the rear, form squadron.	The leading division by order wheels to the left about and *halts*. The others *wheel round* the *leading one*, and successively join on its right. The officer bringing his division up in front of the left file, and then shifting to his post which his coverer has preserved.
From the right of half Squadrons to the front, File.	A Caution.
March!	The leaders of the rear rank move up to the front rank leaders, and both ranks file to the front from the named flanks, the standard leading the left half squadron, the rear rank is the breadth of a horse distant from and dressed to its front rank: quarter-master, &c. follow the files.—Leaders dress, and preserve distances from the left; commanding officer is with the standard half squadron.
Halt!	When sufficiently advanced, halt.
Front form Squadron.	A caution immediately given.

The rear rank leaders cover the front rank leaders, who, with the standard, halt and are in a line.—
Each

MARCH!	Each rank forms up at the fame time, file after file, to its proper leader, and looks to its formed flank; when the whole are up, the fquadron will receive the word, center drefs! and correct any inaccuracy that may exift.
FROM THE LEFT OF HALF SQUADRONS TO THE REAR, FILE!	A caution—when one of the half fquadrons difengages by reining back.
MARCH!	The leaders turn to the rear, and the front rank leaders move up to the rear rank ones, the ftandard in front of its proper half fquadron (the right): quartermafters and trumpets follow their refpective half fquadrons. Leaders drefs and preferve diftances from the right.
TO THE REAR FORM SQUADRON!	The front rank leaders double round the rear rank leaders; place themfelves before them, and together with the ftandard halt.— Both ranks follow their leaders and form up at the fame time; when the whole are up, the fquadron will receive the word—*Center Drefs!*
FROM CENTER OF SQUADRON TO THE FRONT, FILE.	A Caution.
MARCH!	The ftandard, its coverer, and the four center files advance in front. The reft of the fquadron follow in file, till the whole is in four files: the commanding officer leads: the quarter mafter, &c. are in the rear;—dreffing and diftances

{ tances are taken from the ſtandards by the firſt four men.

The followers of the files attend to their leaders, at the fame time that each four may be dreſſed to the right. The double files are feparated a horfe's breadth, if they cover their leaders.

HALT! { When the leader arrives at the intended line.

FRONT FORM SQUADRON. } A Caution.

MARCH! { The ſtandards and files on each fide of it ſtand faſt. The reſt of the ſquadron move up to their places, file by file, and dreſs to the ſtandard.

{ SQUADRONS, TO THE RIGHT WHEEL!
  MARCH!—HALT! DRESS!
{ SQUADRONS—RIGHT WHEEL!
  MARCH!—HALT! DRESS!
{ SQUADRONS—RIGHT ABOUT WHEEL!
  MARCH!—HALT! DRESS!   } Squadron Wheelings.
{ SQUADRONS—LEFT WHEEL!
  MARCH!—HALT! DRESS!
{ SQUADRONS—LEFT WHEEL!
  MARCH!—HALT! DRESS!
{ SQUADRON—LEFT ABOUT WHEEL!
  MARCH!—HALT! DRESS!

RETIRE IN LINE.
HALT AND FRONT. } Ranks by Three's.

The general commands are given by the chief of the whole; thoſe of execution are repeated by leaders of ſquadrons.

INSPEC-

INSPECTION, OR REVIEW OF A REGIMENT OF CAVALRY.

The regiment marches to its ground in open column of fuch front as circumftances allow of—Forms on the alignement in clofe order, with intervals equal to one-third of the fquadron. Every individual is at his poft in fquadron, the regiment takes open order in the manner directed. The trumpets aflemble on the right of the regiment in two ranks; and the ftaff, &c. of chaplain, furgeon, mate, are on the right of the trumpets in the line of the front rank, one horfe's length from it, and half a horfe from each other.

In this difpofition, and eyes to the right, the general is awaited. He is to be received with the compliment due to his rank, as fet forth in the regulations of military honours. On this occafion the fenior officers are at the head of fquadrons, and the commanding officer of the regiment is one horfe's length before the center of the whole.

A point is to be originally marked, about one hundred and fifty yards in front of the center of the regiment, where the general is fuppofed to take his ftation. But although he may choofe to quit that pofition, ftill that fpot is to be confidered as the point to work upon, and to which all movements and formations are relative.

Receiving the General.

DRAW SWORDS! { When the reviewing general prefents himfelf before the center, or before any part of the regiment (or line) the whole DRAW SWORDS, at three motions, the officers coming down at the laft motion to the pofition of the falute, in which fituation

{ ation they make a sufficient pause, and then recover it with the commanding officer. During this operation the whole of the trumpets sound, according to the rank of the general, and standards only salute such persons, as from rank and regulation, are entitled to that honour.

The general then goes towards the right, (accompanied by the commanding officer) and the whole remain steady, without paying any further compliment while he passes along the regiment, during which time music will play or trumpets sound, and they will cease when the general has returned to the right flank of the regiment, and is going away from it.

Eyes left. { When the general turns the left of the left squadron, and passes betwixt the ranks, that squadron turns eyes to the left, as does each of the others, as he approaches them.

Eyes Right! Slope Swords! { When the general is going from the regiment, each squadron dresses to the right, and slopes swords.

Rear Rank, take close order! rch! { While the general is proceeding to place himself in the front, this command will be given, and the regiment prepares to march past. On this particular occasion the officers will be cautioned not to alter their situations, but to remain as at Order.

Marching past.

{ The general having taken his position, the regiment is ordered to wheel

THREE'S RIGHT WHEEL! MARCH! HALT, DRESS!	wheel to the right, ranks by three's: all the officers, &c. face to the right, and each as in a line of a rank of fixes. Trumpeters wheel into one rank, and the staff of surgeon, chaplain, &c. do not march paft.
MARCH!	To the flank, and in the continuation of the former front, which is marked accordingly.
RIGHT SHOULDERS FORWARD! FORWARD!	When the head of the regiment is about two hundred yards from where its center ftood, it will be led circling on a moveable pivot into a new direction, and march down perpendicular to the line on which it is to pafs the general, the head of each fquadron changing direction where the front one does.
HALF SQUADRON! HALT! WHEEL UP! HALT, DRESS! MARCH! EYES RIGHT! TAKE ORDER!	When the head of the leading fquadron arrives within five yards of the line on which it is to pafs the general, the feveral words to form the right half of that fquadron, and drefs to the right, are given rapidly and fucceffively: officers, trumpets and men front, and when the half fquadron has moved on twenty yards, the command is given to take order; the trumpets nimbly move forward, and place themfelves in two ranks before the commanding officer, and found a march. The farriers are a horfe's length behind the center of their troops, and the quarter-mafters behind the farriers.

In this manner, each half fquadron clears the ground for its fucceeding one, which performs the fame operation preparatory to pafling.

	of the troops have, in the fame manner, filed paſt, formed up, and are cloſed up in its rear in column, at quarter diſtance.
MARCH!	Juſt before the rear troops have cloſed up, and ſo as that the laſt one may not make any unneceſſary pauſe on the ground, the leading one will be put in motion, and each ſucceſſively will follow it in open column, when it acquires its proper diſtance.
Left Wheel! *Halt, Dreſs!* *March!* *Left Wheel!* *Halt, Dreſs!* *March!*	The leading half ſquadron will wheel to the left, and proceed to the flank of the ground on which the line is to form; it will there again wheel to the left, and march in the alignement, till it arrives at the right flank of the ground followed by the others in open column.
HALT! WHEEL INTO LINE! MARCH! HALT, DRESS!	The whole will then be ordered to halt and wheel into line.

Should a regiment not be directed to file paſt, it will, after paſſing by half ſquadrons, enter the alignement, and form upon it.

SLOPE SWORDS! CARRY SWORDS!	In general ſwords will be carried with the blade reſting on the hollow of the ſhoulder, and by the word SLOPE SWORDS! On other ordered occaſions, and in parade they will be carried upright at the word CARRY SWORDS!

The regiment being now formed on their original ground, about one hundred and fifty yards from the general, will prepare to perform the sword exercise as follows:

SWORD EXERCISE.

1st, *The Six Divisions in Line.*
2d, *The Six Divisions in Speed.*
3d, *The Attack and Defence in Speed.*

The sword exercise performed in line, will be executed by the whole regiment, and the other movements by only one division from each squadron.

The Six Divisions in Line.

It is not necessary herein to specify the words of command requisite to be given, in order to put a regiment through the exercise; as the opening of ranks and doubling of files, are according to the mode laid down in the drill practice, and the whole being executed by flugelman, the commanding officer will have only to particularize each division of movement, after which he will form up the doubling files, and close ranks.

The Six Divisions in Speed.

DIVISIONS TO THE FRONT FORM. { The ranks being closed, the divisions are to be performed by those men who are previously appointed in each squadron, moving forward on the word march, forming at three horses' length in front of their respective squadrons, and dressing by the right.

In order to perform the exercise in speed, it will be requisite to form the four divisions in two lines, on each flank

flank of the regiment, with the whole fronting inwards. The two divisions of the left wing will be drawn up opposite to the intervals of the division, upon the right and one subaltern will accompany each division. The range between the two lines should not be less than one hundred and fifty yards, and the distances of the divisions sufficiently great, to guard against any possibility of the opposing parties riding against each other.

RANKS BY THREE'S WHEEL OUTWARDS.

MARCH!

HALT! DRESS!
MARCH! TROT!

{ The divisions being formed in front of the line and told off in ranks by three's, the commanding officer will direct them to wheel outwards, and upon the word march, the two divisions of the right wing will wheel to the right, and those of the left in the opposite direction. As soon as they are halted, they will again get the words march and trot, on which they will trot off beyond the flanks of the regiment, and wheel into their new alignement.

WHEEL UP!
HALT! DRESS!

{ As each division arrives on its ground, it is to halt, and wait for the commanding officer's order to wheel up.

When thus formed, the division of the third squadron will be opposite the interval of the two right divisions, with the fourth division upon its left.

PERFORM THE SIX DIVISIONS OF MOVEMENTS IN SPEED.

{ On receiving the caution to perform in speed, the right and left file of the front rank will move forward a horse's length in front of their respective divisions, to be in readiness to spring forward upon the division being specified, at the same time the flanks are to be kept complete by passaging from the center of the rank.

FIRST DIVISION. {　The advanced files of each division will have their horses well in hand, and at the word DIVISION, move forward at an eafy gallop, increafing their fpeed gradually; each file is to direct his horfe in a right line to the front.

Thofe of the right wing, on arriving at the extremity of the range, will form to the rear of the third and fourth divifions, whilft thofe of the left wing will form in the intervals; by which means when the exercife is completed, the four divifions will be immediately oppofite each other.

Attention muft be paid to regulate the time requifite between each motion, according to the extent of ground, as every divifion of movement fhould begin and conclude at the oppofite extremity of the range.

The whole are executed according to the directions given for performing the firft divifion.

The Attack and Defence in Speed.

The attack and defence in fpeed, will confift of divifions filing fucceffively paft the general; the front and rear files attacking and defending alternately, which having done, they will return by the rear of the regiment to their places in fquadron.

On receiving the order to attack and defend in fpeed; the firft divifion of the right wing will file from its left by two's, the rear file commencing the attack on the front file, according to the mode pointed out in drill practice.

They are to move at a pace, rather exceeding half fpeed, taking care to ride in a right line to the oppofite end of the range, where the attack will ceafe; their fwords are immediately to be floped, the files to drefs, and at a gentle trot, wheel round the right flank of the regiment,

regiment, to their places in fquadron. The files will fucceed each other at the diftance of five horfes' lengths, till both divifions of the right wing have fucceffively rode paft the general.

Attention muft be paid that they all move off from the fame ground, which is pointed out by the leading files.

LEFT WING, BY YOUR RIGHT, ATTACK AND DEFEND.
{ The divifions of the left wing will file off from the right, and are in their turns to obferve the rules laid down for the divifions preceding, with this difference, that as their courfe is to be left, they will wheel round the left wing of the regiment to their places in fquadron.

The regiment remains formed at clofe order, ready for evolutions, movements or attacks, as ordered.

Whatever part of the evolutions are performed, they muft be arranged fo as to follow each other with propriety on the ground before the reviewing general.

Evolutions.

Squadron Officer Squadron Officer Squadron Officer Squadron Officer

F Rank
R Rank

Commanding Officer

Serrefile and Supernumerary Officers.

Reviewing Officer

Formation of a Regiment for Exercise. Plate I.

A REGIMENT is formed for exercise at close order. Squadron officers are a horse's length in front of the standard, supernumerary officers and serjeants, quartermasters and trumpeters, are in the rear of the troops, in a line, at two horses distance from the rear rank, and their business is to attend to the movements of the squadron, and particularly to the rear rank.

MOVEMENTS AND ATTACKS.

1. The line is formed about one hundred yards from the general.

The open column of divisions trots past the general, and again forms in line on the ground it quitted.
{
The column of divisions is formed by the wheeling back of divisions. The column passes and takes up its ground at a trot. The flank leaders do not quit the pivot flanks, but they may order their divisions to turn their eyes to the right during the instant of passing.

Change

Plate II. *Change of Position on the left Flank, by throwing back the Right the Eighth of the Circle.*

2. IN the change of position from A to B, the left half fquadron of pofition A is wheeled by its leader into the new alignement B, which alignement is given by the mounted figures 1, 2.

The other half fquadrons are in the mean time put about by three's, and the commanding officer wheels them to the right, in the degree requifite. During which the alignement B is prolonged by the markers of fquadrons, who fucceffively arrive at, and place themfelves on the new alignement, which is terminated by marker 3.

Vide Section 43. The round dots fhew the pofts of half fquadron leaders, and the blunted arrows denote the markers of the wheel in echellon, as reprefented by figure F. The dotted lines fhew the march of the leaders, and the pointed arrow the front to which they move.

The echellon G is the diftance where each divifion is, in its turn, wheeled into the new direction, by bringing the left fhoulders forward. As each half fquadron arrives on the new line, it halts, fronts, and dreffes.

The mounted figures are the fquadron markers, who prolong the line, and place themfelves on the outward flanks of their refpective fquadrons.

Squadron officers correct the line from the left flank.

PLATE II

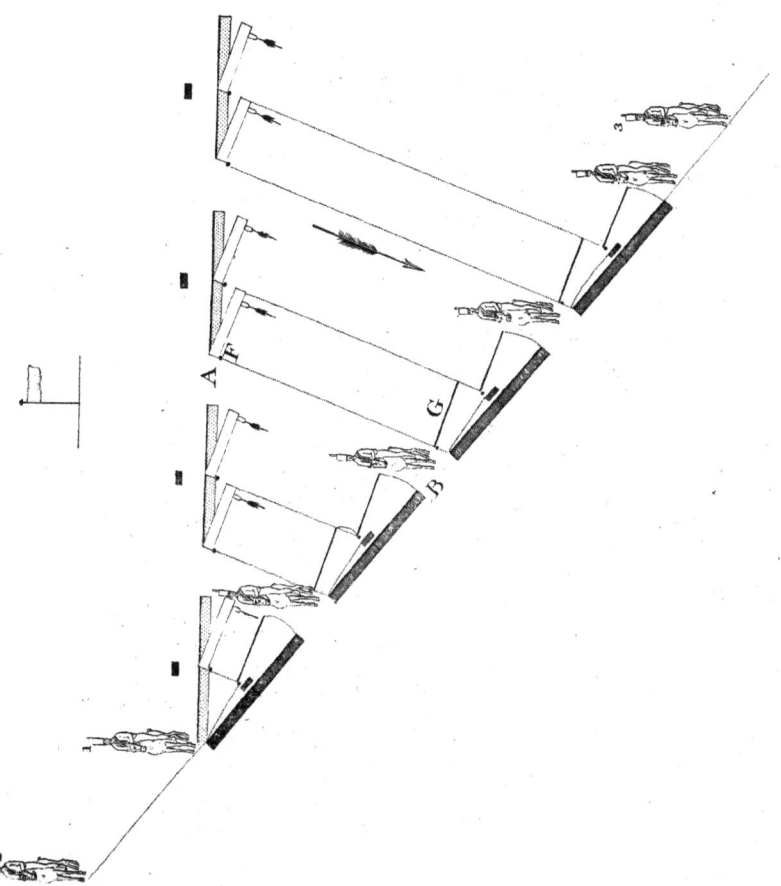

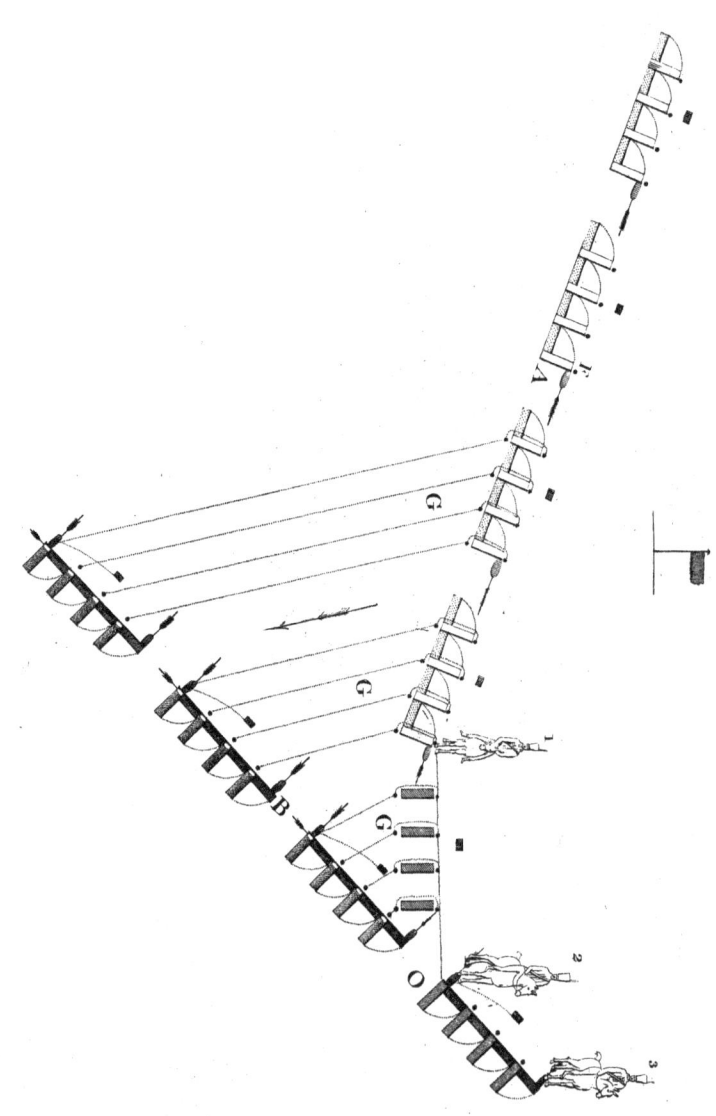

Change of Position in Open Column, the Left thrown back. Plate III.

3. THE position A is the same which terminated the manœuvre No. 2, and B is the new alignement to be taken up.

EXAMPLE.

The commanding officer breaks the line A, into a column of divisions from the right, as represented in column F. When the column is put in motion, marker No. 1 turns the head of the column to the left.

Marker No. 2 directs it again to the left, and the marker No. 3 prolongs the line of the new direction B.

The first squadron having arrived on the alignement B, the column is halted.

The remaining three squadrons G G G are wheeled by the commanding officer, ranks by three's to the right, and the leaders of divisions, shifting at the same time to that flank, will, at the word *march*, conduct their divisions into the column O, where they halt and front them, and from whence they are afterwards wheeled to the left into position B. Vide Section 17.

The blunt arrows in column F give the square of the wheel; the small arrows in column O are the markers of divisions sent out to take up the direction in the new column.

The markers for wheeling into the line B are represented by blunt arrows on the flanks of squadrons.

The column O being wheeled into line, the squadron officers will shift to the left flank, and dress their squadron from that point.

Plate IV. *Change of Position on the Right Flank, the Left brought forward.*

4. THE position A is the same which terminated the manœuvre No. 3, and B is the new alignement to be taken up.

The right half squadron of position A is wheeled by its leader into the new direction B, which alignement is taken up by the markers 1, 2. The remaining half squadrons are by the commanding officer wheeled to the right in the degree requisite, as represented by the echellon F. The leaders will then shift to the inward flank, and at the word *march!* move forward to the position B, the squadron markers taking care at the same time to advance at an encreased pace, in order to prolong the alignement, which is terminated by the marker 3.

Vide Section 43.

The echellon G denotes the wheeling of half squadrons into the alignement B, by bringing the left shoulders forward.

Squadron officers will dress their squadrons from the right.

PLATE IV

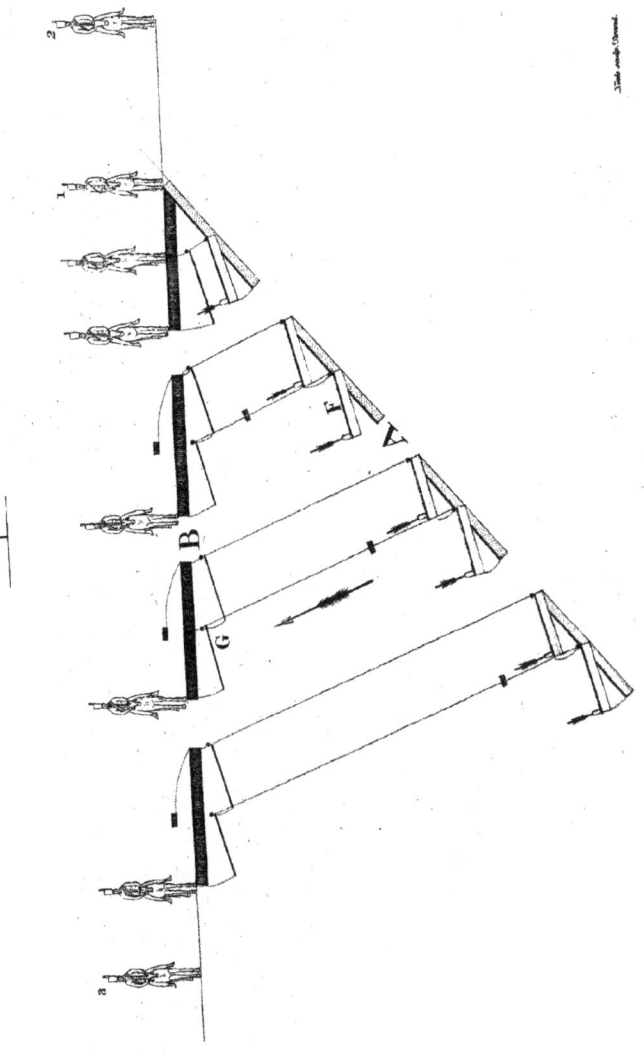

PLATE V

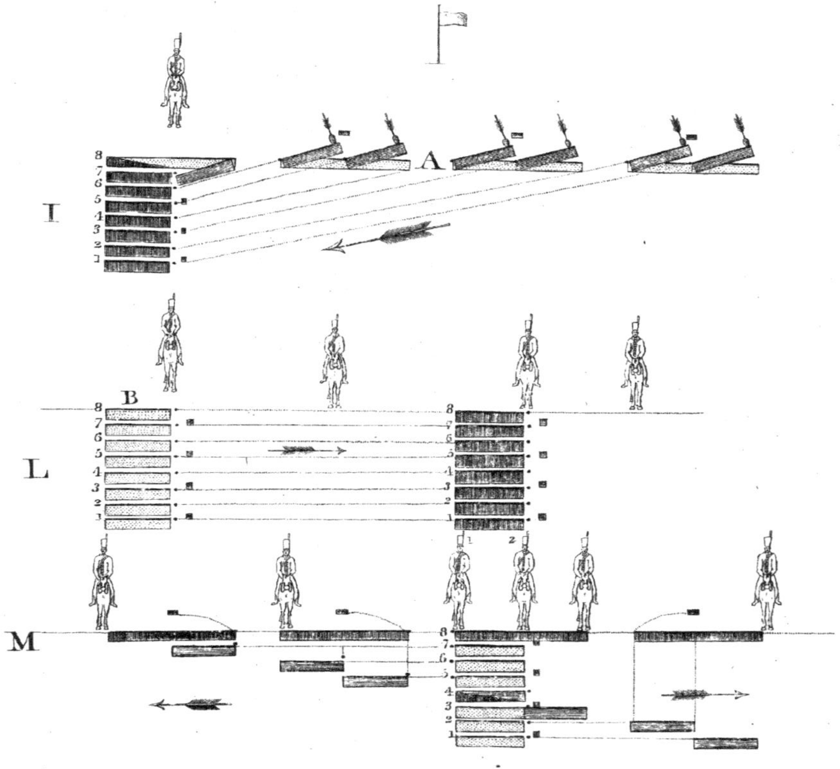

The close Column is formed, marches and deploys into Line.

Plate V.

5. IN plate No. 5, there are three movements, as diftinguifhed by the initials I. L. M. The firft movement (I) confifts in forming a column behind the left half fquadron; the fecond movement (L) reprefents the flank march of the column to the right. In the third movement (M) the column deploys, and forms line on a central half fquadron.

On movement (I), the line A being ordered by the commanding officer to form clofe column to the rear of the left half fquadron, the left half fquadron officer will place the marker No. 1. The line is then wheeled by half fquadrons, an eighth to the left (half fquadron No. 7. excepted, which difengages by reining back.) The whole will afterwards take ground by three's to the left, when the leaders placing themfelves at the heads of their half fquadrons, are, at the word *march!* to conduct them to the places in column, where they will cover and drefs to the right. Vide Section.

No markers are neceffary to regulate the diftance of half fquadrons in clofe column.

Movement L. The column B is wheeled by the commanding officer, ranks by three's to the right, and marched till it arrives oppofite the general, when he will order it to halt and wheel up. During its flank march, guides are to be fent out, to direct the movement of the column parallel to its proper front. Vide Section 33.

Movement M. A caution being given, to deploy on a central half fquadron, the officer of the named half fquadron fends markers, No. 1, 2, to determine the ground occupied by the front half fquadron, to which he will march whenever his front is clear. Vide Section 37. Example 3.

The commanding officer will then direct the half fquadrons to wheel outwards by three's; that on which the deployment is made ftands faft, thofe to its front wheel

wheel to the left, and thofe in the rear to the oppofite hand.

The officers fhifting to the heads of their half fquadrons will at the word *march!* lead ftraight out, and as each half fquadron arrives parallel to the ground where it is to form on the new line, it will halt, wheel up, and move forward into line.

Squadron markers are to prolong the line as ufual, and officers will drefs their fquadrons from the flank to which they formed.

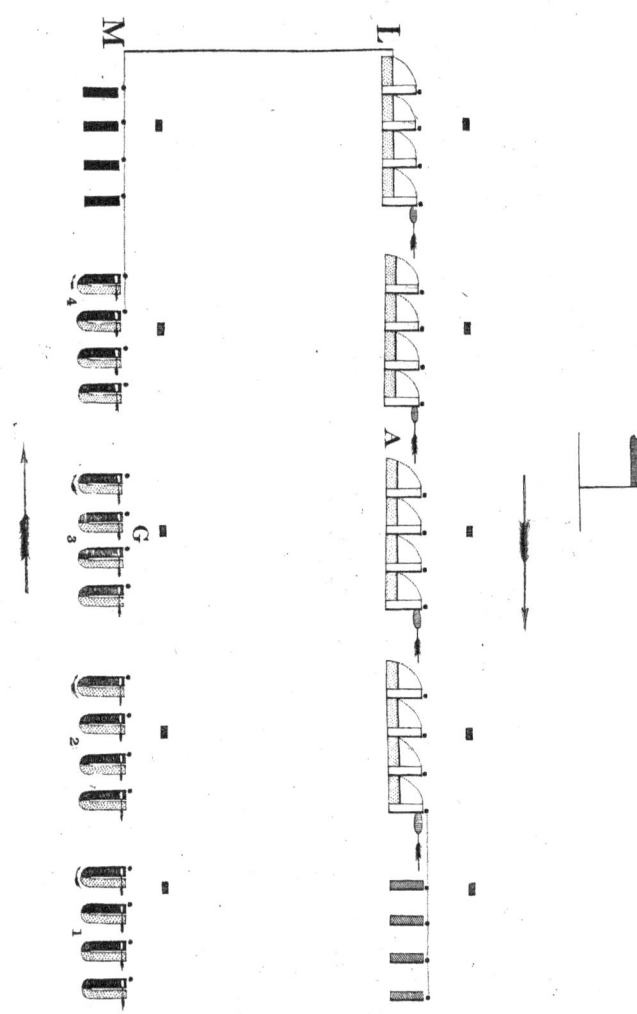

Countermarch of the Divisions of the Open Column.

Plate VI.

6. IN the annexed plate there are two figures, L and M. L represents the line A, broken into a column of divisions, right in front, which column marches the distance of a squadron's length. M represents the countermarch of divisions.

On movement L. In wheeling by divisions, the usual markers for each squadron give the square of the wheel, and when in column, the covering and dressing is to the left.

Movement M. The squadrons 1, 2, 3, 4, of column G, are required to countermarch; and on the commanding officer giving a caution to that effect, a marker, from the right of each division, will immediately go to the left flank, and occupy the officer's place in the division, with this difference, that he turns his horse *to the front intended by the countermarch*, (vide the markers in column G) the officer at the same time shifts to the right of the division, and at the word *March!* the division files from the right, and is conducted by the rear to the marker on the opposite flank, when it receives from the division officer the words *Form, Dress*. The column being formed to the new front, it returns to its former ground, covering and dressing to the right.

Vide Section 27.

In all countermarches by files, the division officer will lead out to the flank, in the degree of one third the front of his division, before he countermarches.

Plate VII. *The open Column changes Position to the Flank, by the Flank March of its Divisions.*

7. THE column G retires by a flank march of its divisions; it then halts in the position of column F, and wheels into the line A.

Vide Section 21.

The column G having received a caution to retire, the divisions will be wheeled by three's to the left, at which time the leaders are to shift by the rear to the head of their divisions, and at the word *March!* retire conducted by the division on the right. When arrived at the distance of two hundred yards from the former ground, the column will be ordered to halt, and wheel up, on which the divisions will wheel by three's to the right; the leaders are then to return to the right flank, to which hand they must cover and dress, ready to wheel into the line A. During the retreat, great attention is to be paid, that the leaders of the divisions dress, and wheeling intervals are properly preserved, from the *right division*, it being the head division of the column when fronted. When the markers 1, 2, are placed, and the caution given to wheel into line, those who direct the square of the wheel immediately aligne themselves on the points thrown out for that purpose; and at the word *March!* the divisions will come rapidly into line, and the officers dress their squadrons from the right flank.

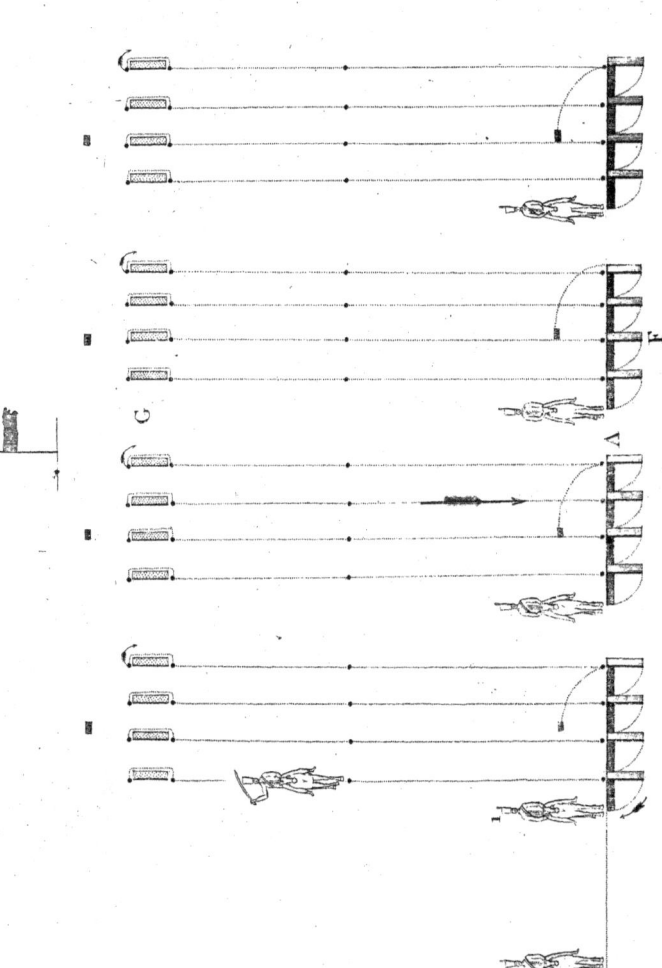

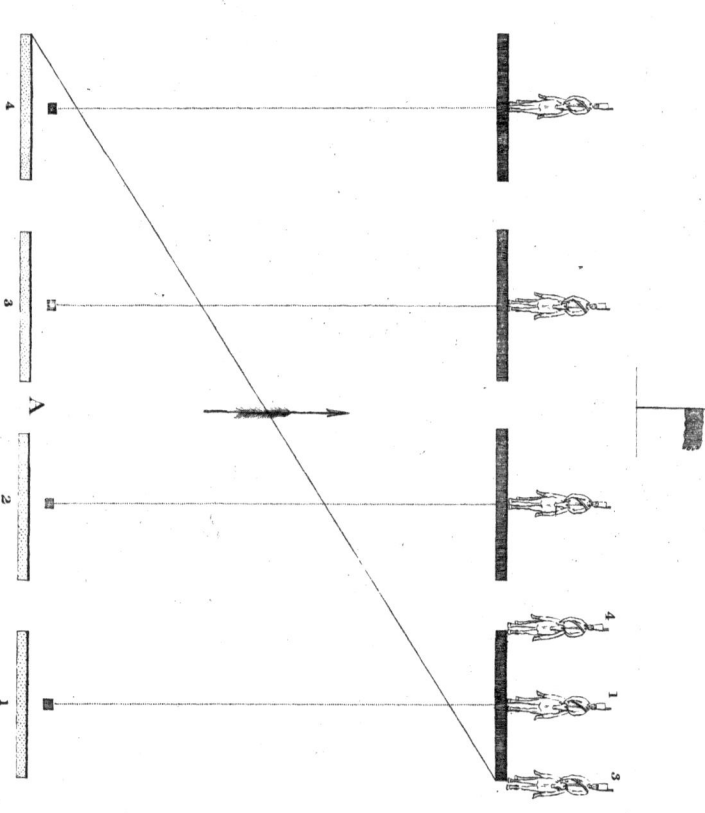

PLATE VIII

Attack by Squadrons successively. Plate VIII.

8. THE line A attacks to the front, by squadrons from the right; each moving when the one preceding it has just finished its attack. They successively arrive and halt in line.

The adjutant places himself in the position of marker No. 1, on whom the right squadron officer will lead his squadron to the charge, which having made, the adjutant will shift to the front of the second squadron for the same purpose, and so successively become the point of direction for each squadron officer. Vide Section 9.

After the charge is completed, flank serjeants (markers 3, 4,) turn out to dress the squadron, which is done from the center.

Plate IX.

The Line retires in Echellon.

9. THE line A retires in echellon of squadrons from the left, and afterwards forms the line B, on the right center squadron.

The commanding officer having given the caution to retire in echellon, of squadrons from the left, the left squadron officer will put his squadron about by three's, and lead in a right line to the rear. As soon as the left squadron is arrived at the distance of thirty yards from the line A, the left center squadron will march; and in like manner, are the other squadrons to move in echellon. When the retreat is made in the degree required, the whole will be halted, and receive orders to form the line on the right center squadron, which squadron is instantly fronted, and dressed by the markers 1, 2.

Vide page 57.

The remaining squadrons are conducted by their leaders into line (which line is succesively prolonged by the markers on the outer flanks of each squadron, and terminated by the markers 3 and 4): The right squadron moves up and fronts on the new line, and the two left squadrons instantly come about, and move forward to their markers. As each squadron arrives on the new line, the officers dress their squadrons on the first formed squadron.

PLATE IX

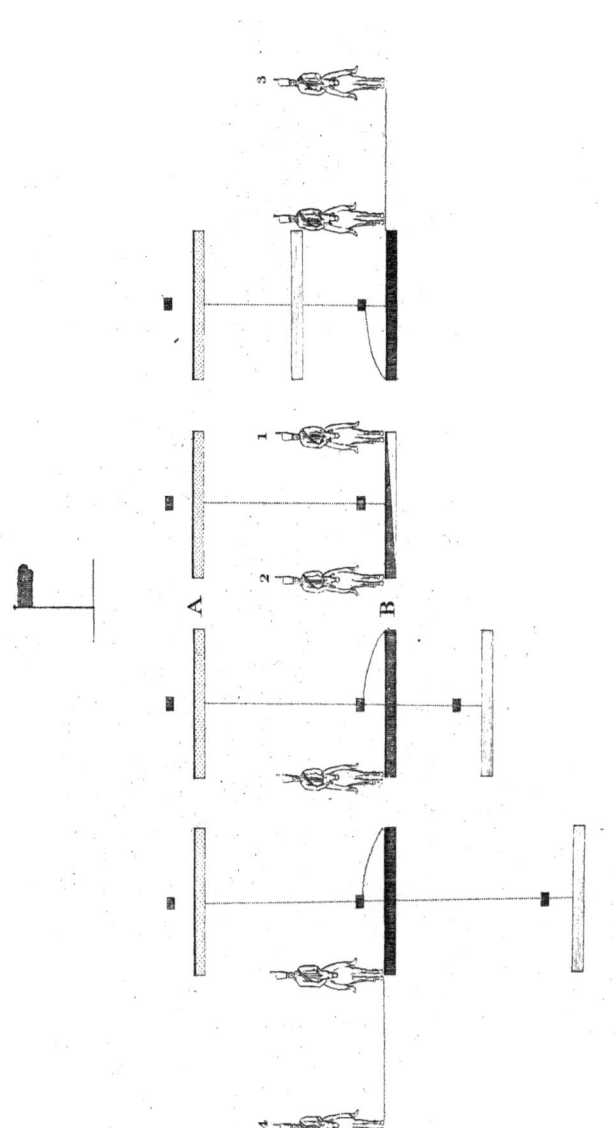

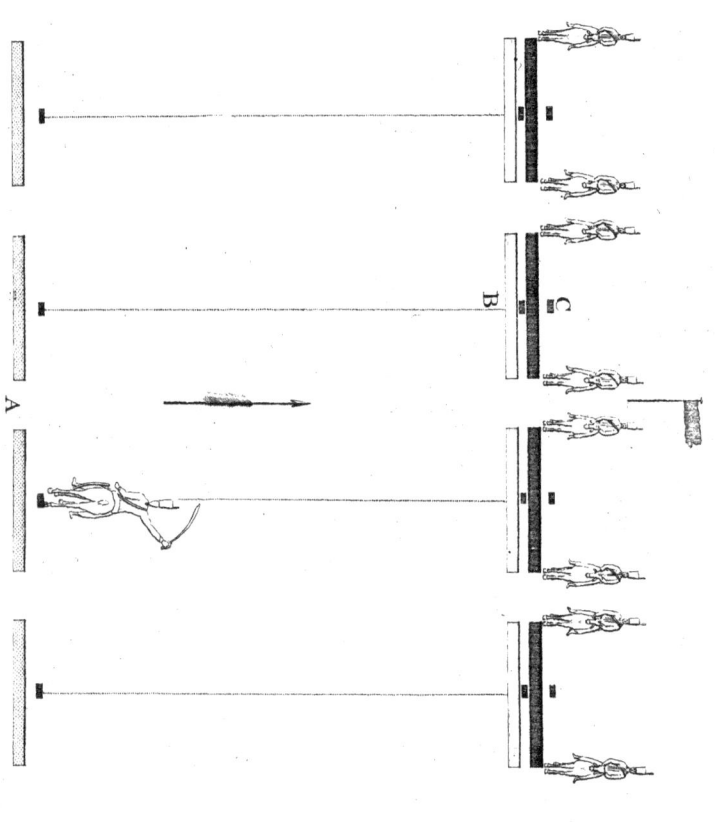

The Line attacks to the Front.   Plate X.

10. THE line A advances to the charge. B is the   Vide Sec-
position to which it charges, and C the alignement   tion 45.
taken up after the charge is made.

The line A advances to the charge, and the right center squadron being named as the squadron of direction, it must be the particular care of its leader to move on in a direct line to his front; and in order to preserve that uniformity of motion, which insures a steady charge, he must gradually increase his pace, till he arrives at the charge in speed.

The line is halted by the commanding officer on the position B, and if a correct dressing is required, markers 1 and 2 move forward from the squadron of direction, and take up the alignement C, which is immediately prolonged by the markers of the other squadrons. Each squadron moves up as its respective markers are placed, and dresses on the squadron of direction.

Should the next movements not be performed, the line will retire after the charge, about one hundred yards, ranks by three's, then halt, front, advance at open order, and general salute.

Plate XI. *The Line retires, and forms two Columns.*

11. THE annexed plate reprefents three figures, diftinguifhed by the letters I, L, M. Part of the line I, forms a column of half fquadrons, behind the adjoining half fquadron, at quarter diftance.

L reprefents the retiring of the line; and in M is feen the clofing up of the column, and the two left half fquadrons formed behind their adjoining one.

On movement I. The two fquadrons on the right having been cautioned to form a column of half fquadrons, at quarter diftance, behind the adjoining half fquadron H, the marker 1, is to be immediately placed; the commanding officer will then wheel the right wing by half fquadrons an eighth to the left, and afterwards by three's to the fame hand.

The leaders will place themfelves at the head of their half fquadrons, and at the word *march!* conduct them into column, where they are to cover and drefs by the right.

Movement L. When the column is formed, the whole will be put about by three's, and retire to the pofition L, where the commanding officer will halt and front them.

Movement M. The column L having fronted, it will be ordered to clofe to the front, as reprefented in figure M. The left fquadron is then wheeled by half fquadrons, an eighth to the right, and afterwards take ground by three's to the right, when at the word *march!* they will be conducted into column, behind the adjoining half fquadron B, where they are to cover and drefs to the left.

Attack

PLATE XI

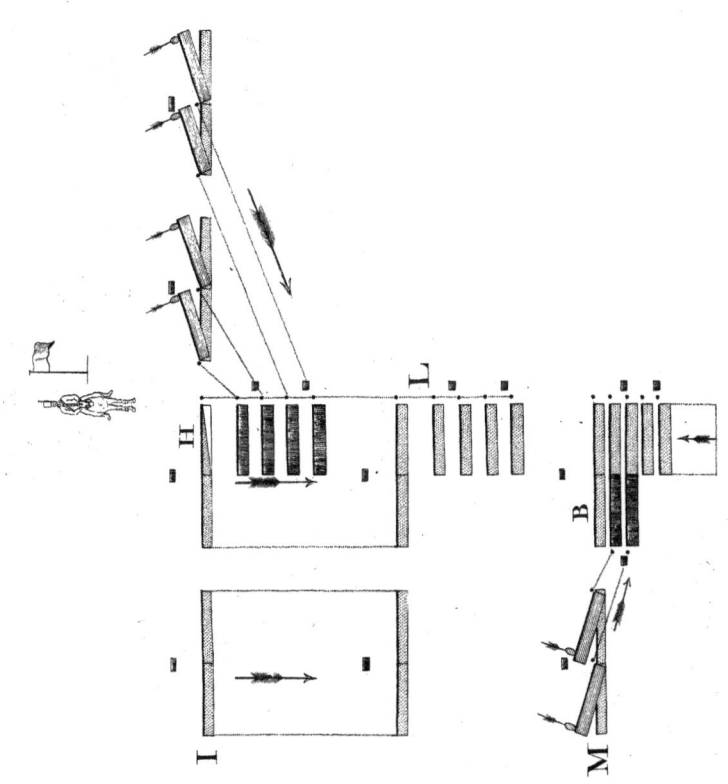

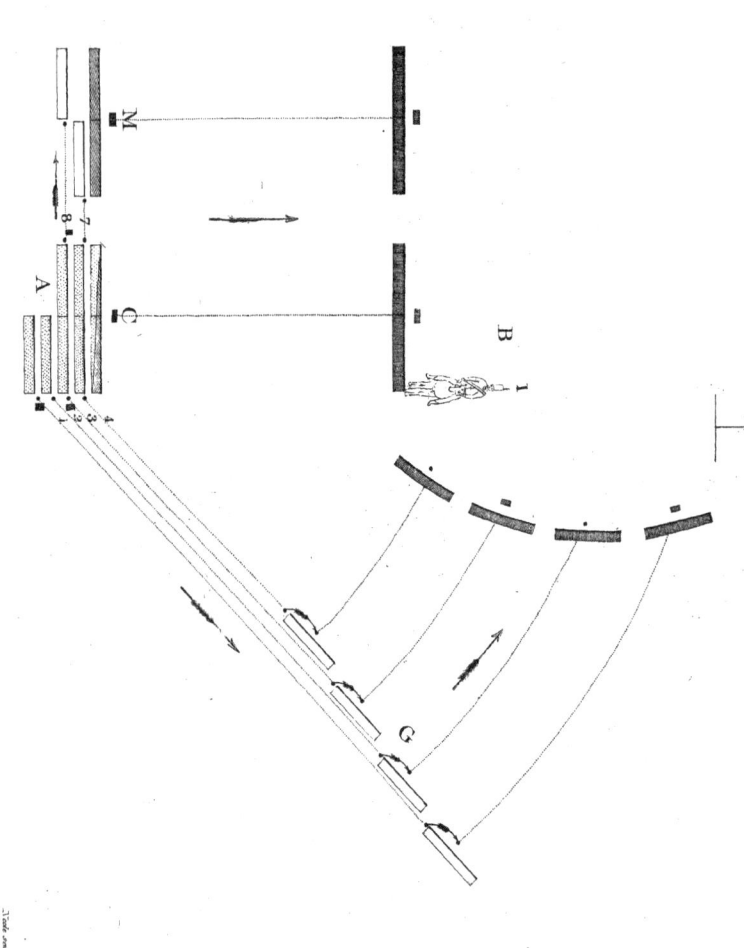

Attack of the Enemy in Front and Flank. Plate XII.

12. THE column A deploys, during which the front squadron C moves forward; the left squadron forms to the front, whilst the two squadrons on the right take the oblique direction G, from whence the whole will charge to the position B, the movements of the front attack corresponding with that of the flank. *Vide Section 50.*

The column having received a caution to attack in front and flank, the adjutant will place himself opposite the right flank of the column, in the situation of marker No. 1. The commanding officer then wheels half squadrons by three's outwards, which having done, at the word *march!* the whole will move together. The formed squadron C moves forward. Half squadrons 7, 8, deploy and form squadron M, dressing by the right. Half squadrons 1, 2, 3, 4, composing the right wing, lead in the oblique direction G; when having gone one hundred yards, or more, the leading half squadron 4, wheels up and dresses, so as to be nearly perpendicular to its charging point marker 1; it then advances, and the other half squadrons, 3, 2, 1, proceed to the flank, and successively halt, wheel, and come up to the right of each other; during which, the movements of the left wing (squadrons C and M) are carried on, and made to correspond to this flank attack.

Plate XIII. *Retire in two Lines by alternate Half Squadrons.*

13. THE regiment A A retires by alternate half fquadrons in two lines, to pofition B, and during the retreat, the half fquadrons of the right wing gradually gain their pofition in line.

Vide Section 47.

The regiment is cautioned to retire in two lines. The right half fquadrons (1, 3, 5, 7,) to compofe the firft line.

The fecond line ftands faft. The firft line is put about by three's, and at the word *march!* will retreat towards the pofition B, dreffing by a named half fquadron.

The retiring line having marched a given diftance, will receive orders to *halt!* and *front!* which orders ferve as a fignal to the fecond line to begin its retreat, in the fame manner, through its proper intervals.

The alternate retreat is thus continued, till the line has attained the pofition B.

---

14. GENERAL SALUTE.

REAR ranks are opened, and the regiment advances in parade order, trumpets founding, &c. &c. within thirty yards of the general.

HALT!

GENERAL SALUTE.

PLATE XIII

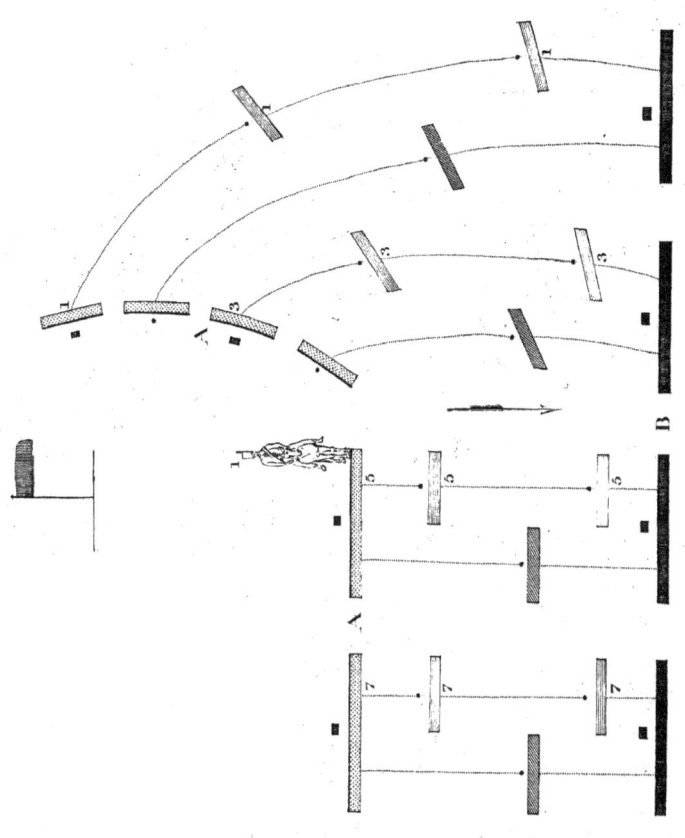

ADDITIONAL INSTRUCTIONS.

The evolutions, movements and attacks are such as seem essential for the general practice of the regiment. The whole of them may not be required at any one exercise or inspection, and such therefore as are to be performed (always including the first seven movements if space allows), must be arranged and connected according to the extent of, and circumstances of the ground on which they are to be exhibited; and on the smallest spot such changes of position may be made, as will clearly shew what may be expected from the body in more extended situations.

No improper pauses should be made betwixt the connected parts of the same movement. The detached points necessary in formations should be timeously prepared and given by the persons who are so ordered.

Commanding officers are moveable according to circumstances, and should by no means consider the center as their general post in exercise or movements, or expect by the exertion of one voice, from one fixed situation, to command and direct the whole; their presence is more frequently required near one or other flank; in general they should be at the conducting point of movement, or formation, and to that address their orders by voice or message, for if that point be led, or placed in the direction it should take, there is little danger of the parts of the body, not properly, and successively conforming to it.

The words of command as marked in the margin and those at the end of the book, for the movements, are to be strictly made use of, and no other substituted in their room; in the quick movements, and manœuvres of cavalry they must be rapidly given.

In

In paſſing by in half-ſquadrons at open ranks, the commander of the ſquadron will be in front of his leading half-ſquadron, covered by the ſtandard with which the other officers of the half-ſquadron dreſs. In the ſecond half-ſquadron all its officers are in front, and in one line. The trumpets are all in front of the regiment, and when they have paſſed, wheel quickly round, and remain poſted oppoſite his Majeſty, and ſound till the regiment has paſſed, when they ceaſe.

In paſſing by half-ſquadrons or diviſions, at cloſe ranks, the ſtandard may take the center of the front rank of the leading one. The commanding officer is before it, other officers are at their ſquadron-poſts, and care is taken that there ſhall be an officer on each paſſing flank.

At the drawing of ſwords, and general ſalute, on his Majeſty's approach, the trumpets all ſound the parade march. When his Majeſty paſſes along the line, the regiment ſounds its own march, or ſuch other as ſhall be ordered.

The trumpet flouriſh, in drawing ſwords, is uſed regimentally on their own ground, and is the ſounding uſed in receiving a major-general; it is repeated twice for a lieutenant-general, and to all ſuperior generals the march is ſounded.

In parade, to receive his Majeſty, or the commanding general, the trumpets are aſſembled on the right of their regiments in two ranks, and the ſtaff beyond them. The ſtaff does not march paſt.

On all occaſions of exerciſe and manœuvre, trumpets are behind their troops and ſquadrons, unleſs otherwiſe detached.

In general, a regiment ſhould manœuvre before the
perſon

perfon infpecting it, fo as to terminate many of its movements and formations within twenty or thirty yards of where he ftands.

SKIRMISHING.

Skirmifhers, or ranks detached to fire, fhould be at leaft two hundred yards from the fquadron, if the ground allows.

When any part of the fquadron is detached to attack, or fire, the remainder always fupport with drawn fwords.

The ftandard always remains with the body of the fquadron, and never moves with any detached part of it. Single fkirmifhers can take the fureft aim, with their carbines, to the left; they will alfo occafionally fire to the front, and to the right; but muft take the greateft care not to hit, or burn the horfe's head, or at that time to fpur him.

Skirmifhers fhould always retire in proportion as the fquadron retires; cover the front of it, at one hundred and fifty yards diftance at leaft, and manage fo as to keep up a conftant fire, nor fhould they ever remain in a clufter to become a mark. All firings are beft performed on the move; and it is unneceffary to halt for that purpofe only. Whenever the line retires, fkirmifhers fhould be ordered out to cover the retreat, and fhould join at the firft fignal. No fkirmifhers ever to fire but when advanced to the front, and never when behind other men. Skirmifhers if not ordered to join, retire through the intervals when the line advances to charge; and form and fupport. The retreat of the line fhould be generally made at a brifk pace; to get quick off the ground, and no time ought to be loft in giving the proper fignal, or word of command. In detached open ranks, the officer commanding the rank is always moft conveniently placed in the center of it, and the men drefs and are directed by him.

Skirmifhers

Skirmishers are to be very attentive and alert in instantly obeying the signals made for their direction, particularly those of ceasing to fire, and of rallying to their divisions: and when the signal for calling in skirmishers is succeeded by that of rally made from the main body, the divisions themselves return quickly, even though they should not then be joined by their detached men.

Skirmishing detachments are usually made of a flank division or sub-division (or their front or rear ranks only) of squadrons. *In advancing*, these are rapidly sent forward about one hundred and fifty yards in front of their respective squadrons, from which *body* are detached three or more *files*, one hundred yards still further forward, where they halt fronting the enemy. The outward flank files of this advanced detachment stand fast, while the others file inwards towards each other, in order to divide the ground and cover the front of the reserve as well as that of their squadron.

This operation, followed by all the detachments from the squadrons, will effectually cover the front of a corps.

In this situation the advanced line of skirmishers are to have their pistols or carbines at the recover; (if pistols, then the sword is to be slung to the wrist). The rear rank men will invariably cover those of the front rank; while the front rank advances in skirmishing.

When the front rank has fired, the rear rank is brought forward in its turn, by the officer or serjeant who is stationed between the two lines, in order to see and direct the rear one. The advancing line will regulate its pace by his, and will halt and dress by him when he halts.

For this movement of the rear line to the front, the officer or serjeant commanding gives the word, *Rear rank forward!* accompanied by a wide signal with his sword; the rear rank passes the front line fifty yards, when the rear rank begins to load.

The files of the front line must attend particularly to the circumstance of not firing till the rear line (their support), is loaded. On this principle will each rank

pass

pafs through the other, fucceffively firing and fupporting each other. Each man of the front rank, either in advancing or retiring, will pafs his rear rank man to his right, whilft the rear rank men under the fame circumftances pafs on the left. This regulation prevents any two men paffing through the fame interval.

In retiring. When the rank next the enemy has fired, it retires by word of command, affifted by fignal, and forms fifty yards in rear of thofe by whom they were before covered, and as they front immediately begin to load. The inftant the retiring line has paft the fupporting line, the fkirmifhers make a flank movement to each hand for a few paces and back again, in order not to be fixed marks for the enemy's fkirmifhers: at the fame time they are occafionally to halt and fire as they perceive their rear file loaded. Thus the two lines retire through each other fucceffively fronting and fupporting.
——To retire, the word of command is, *about!*—to face the enemy, *Front!*—In retiring, each file turns his horfe to the left about:—in fronting he brings him to the right about:

Whenever fkirmifhers are called in they form to the referve, returning their piftols and floping their fwords, without waiting for any word of command to do fo.— The officer commanding the divifion puts the divifion about by three's, and returns to his place in fquadron. But fhould the line be advancing to the charge, the divifions, if they can, will gain their place in fquadron and join in the charge; or otherwife they will form behind the fquadron and fupport.

When a line or column moves to a flank, and that fkirmifhers are out, they are not to wait an order for them to conform to that movement of the main body, but will cover that flank which may be expofed to the enemy; for inftance: if the movement of the line is to the right, then the left of the line of march muft be covered; and the reverfe is to be obferved in the oppofite cafe.

The fkirmifhers covering a flank movement will march in fingle file, the rear rank man immediately behind his front rank file, judging the diftance fo as completely to cover the fquadron, which fhould be outflanked

flanked by its fkirmifhers rather than otherwife. The fame principle of referving the fire with the front line, till the rear fupport is loaded, muft equally be attended to in flank movements, as in the cafes of advancing or retiring; but in the practice there is this difference, that a front file in a flank movement cannot fee when his referve has loaded, therefore it is to be announced to him by word, *Ready!* when he will fire at difcretion.

Advanced guards and patroles on the flanks, are in all fituations effential to guard againft a furprize, and the ftrength of both muft depend upon that of the body in march, and other circumftances. Although in general, the movement of an army is fo covered by light troops, and advanced corps, that every other precaution feems unneceffary; yet no column or detached body is to neglect this military precaution for its peculiar fafety; and the conduct of the advanced guard of an officer and forty or fifty men, may fhew the general principles on which more confiderable bodies are to act on the fame fervice.

The advanced guard in general marches about two hundred yards in front of the column, regiment, or fmaller body; but the diftance muft depend on the nature of the country, which, when woody, makes it neceffary to remain nearer the main body, than when it is free from inclofures.

From the advanced guard, the officer detaches to his front a ferjeant and twelve men, who are to preferve the fame diftance from the officer's party, that the officer is from the column.

The ferjeant is in like manner to fend two men forward, and detach two others, one on each flank, as fide patroles, who are to keep in a line with thofe men moft in advance. The officer will for the fame purpofe, detach one non-commiffioned officer and four men on each of his flanks. The fide patroles are diftant between three and four hundred yards on the flanks, which diftance varies according to the places they have to examine, and the impediments met with on the march:

they

they are not to lose sight of each other for any length of time, but to take the advantage of every height to look round them, and see that they preserve a corresponding line with each other, and the march of the advanced guard.

The patroles must examine all villages, hollow ways, and woods, that lie in the direction of their march, taking care to reconnoitre from the heights the country below, before they descend into the vallies. As soon as the enemy is perceived, the person who discovers him must fire a pistol to announce it, when the non-commissioned officer of the party will ride to the spot, and having made his observations, send a correct report of what he has seen to the officer, who is to convey it to the officer commanding the column.

It is a necessary precaution to send out side patroles from the column, and likewise a rear guard when it is possible for an enemy to approach in that direction. The rear guard is to be conducted on the same principle directed for the advance.

An out-post having been taken up under a knowledge of the country, its *relief* will be conducted in the following manner:

When arrived at the post, the relief takes place by drawing up behind the old guard, who must be on horseback to receive the new guard. The number of men necessary for the relief of the videts (or sentries), are then to be marched off, and conducted by a non-commissioned officer of the old guard.

The officers attend the relief, and the relieving officer must inform himself of the particular orders of every videt; have pointed out to him how far the videts advance by day, and where retired to at night; whether the enemy appeared during the twenty-four preceding hours, and in what direction: he must ask the names of the villages, and the direction of the roads, which he will compare on the spot with his map: he should know what patroles have been made, to what distance, and how frequent; what posts his flanks communicate with;

with; and in cafe of an attack, the fupport to be expected, and from what quarters: he likewife will inform himfelf of the name of the field officer commanding the line of pofts, and where he is to be found, in order to report to him if neceffary.

The Relief having been made, the new guard will take up the fame ground which the old one occupied.—The men may difmount, but not take off their accoutrements, or be permitted to ftray from their horfes.

The horfes are to be kept conftantly bitted, except when feeding, which muft never exceed one fourth of the number at a time, and at fuch hours as the enemy are leaft likely to appear.

No perfon is to be allowed to pafs the out-poft without producing an order from the general commanding in chief; nor is any perfon to be permitted to approach the guard, under a pretence of felling provifions, or for any other purpofe, without the officer firft being informed of it.

The officer muft vifit his videts frequently by day, and keep conftant patroles moving by night. The appearance of any enemy in force, their approach by night, or the defertion of any of the videts with the watchword, muft not only be immediately communicated to the field officer commanding, but to the pofts on the right and left, and the *counterfign* be changed to guard againft furprize.

Before fun fet, if not done in the early part of the day, the officer fhould reconnoitre in front of his poft; for which purpofe he muft determine from his map the route to be taken, and with fifteen or twenty of his guard, he will advance on the fame principle of caution pointed out for an advanced guard; only that the party muft be concentrated, the force being lefs confiderable and unfupported. An officer on out-poft duty fhould be provided with a good glafs, which, in reconnoitring, will always be found very ferviceable. Wherever two roads meet, the party fhould halt, till one of the roads is reconnoitred,

reconnoitred, without which it cannot be fafe to proceed on the other.

On duties of patrole or reconoitring parties, the men muft be filent and watchful, and march at open files.

At night, patroles are to be conducted in fmaller bodies than reconnoitring parties; they will direct their march on the different roads leading towards the enemy. Three men are to be advanced in front of the patrole, two of whom may be a hundred yards, and the third man fifty more, in front of them. A caution always requifite to be taken to guard againft furprize.

A non-commiffioned officer, or junior officer, generally conducts the patrole, as the officer commanding muft not leave his guard during the night.

The utmoft filence is neceffary to the fafety of a patrole, and that they fhould march with files very open. The barking of dogs in villages occupied by the enemy, moving of lights, or any noife breaking in on the ftillnefs of the night, are tokens of the enemy being in motion, and to which patroles muft direct their particular attention.

The guard will mount their horfes an hour before funfet, and continue fo till dark; likewife before day-break, and remain mounted till the approach of an enemy may be clearly perceived, or that the relief arrives; which relief generally takes place at day-break, in order to have the guards doubled at the time moft dangerous for furprize.

TRUMPET

TRUMPET DUTY SOUNDINGS.

1. *Reveille*
2. *Stable Call*   For stable duties.
3. *Boots and Saddles*   ⎧ When to turn out on horse-
4. *To Horse*   ⎨ back, for a march, exercise,
                            ⎩ or other duty.

5. *Draw Swords*   ⎧ These soundings begin at the
6. *Return Swords*   ⎨ instants of drawing the sword
                            ⎩ *from*, and returning it *to* the scabbard.

7. *Parade March*
8. *Parade Call*   For assembling on foot
9. *Officers Call*
10. *Serjeants Call*
11. *Trumpeters Call*
12. *Orders*
13. *Dinner Call*   For men, and for officers.
14. *Watering Call*   To turn out in watering order.
15. *Setting the Watch*

These duty soundings, according to situation, are given by one trumpet, or by the whole of the quarter, regiment, or camp.

TRUMPET EXERCISE SOUNDINGS.

16. *March.* — The squadron, regiment or line, being halted, the trumpet of the commander will accompany the word, *The   will advance;* and at the word *March,* the whole will move at a walk.

17. *Trot.*
18. *Gallop.*
19. *Charge.* — When the body is marching at a walk, on the signal to trot, the whole instantly receive the word *Trot,* and change pace immediately. The same is to be observed from the trot to the light *Gallop,* and from the gallop to the *Charge.* During the charge itself, the trumpets of all the squadrons that are charging, may sound.

20. *Halt.* — The whole halt on the word of command. After the halt of a retreating body, the proper command will bring it to its proper front.

21. *Retreat.* — The signal of *Retreat* (which will be often preceded by that of halt) is a general caution for the several words of execution to be given.

22. *Rally.* — The signal to *Rally* may be continued as long as it is necessary, and be repeated by the trumpets of such parts of the body, as are concerned in the operation, till the end is answered.

These signals are given by the chief commander only of the whole body that is exercised, whether of a squadron, regiment, brigade, or a line; they are not repeated by other commanders; they are addressed as cautions to the commanding officers of the parts of such body,

body, not to the men, nor is any movement, or alteration of movement, to take place, but in confequence of the words, *march, trot, gallop,* &c. &c. rapidly and loudly repeated, the inftant the trumpet caution is given.

The fignals of movement are fo fhort, that the words of execution may nearly coincide with them.

Thefe fignals for quick movement, may in regular exercife be given by a perfon who at the inftant of giving them is ftationary; but if he leads the body in motion, it is evident that in the gallop, the charge, and the halt, the voice, and the eye, can only determine, and regulate.

23. *Turn out Skirmifhers.*

This fignal is made by the commander of the whole, if the whole is concerned, otherwife by the commander of fuch part only as is to execute; if one or two fquadrons only, the voice will fuffice. It may be a fignal for purfuers after a charge.

24. *Call in Skirmifhers.*

This fignal is made by the commander of the whole, and repeated by the commander of detachments for the fkirmifhers to join their detachments; or it may originally come from the commander of the detachments. On the fignal to *rally*, the whole join the bodies they were detached from.

25. *Skirmifhers ceafe firing.*

This fignal is made by the commander of the whole, and repeated (or originally made) by the commander of the fupporting detachments, from which the fkirmifhers are advanced.

BUGLE

BUGLE HORN DUTY SOUNDINGS.

1. *Reveille*
2. *Roufe, or turn out*
3. *Dinner call*
4. *Setting the watch*

{ Thefe foundings are different in their notes from thofe of the trumpet, but may be ufed under the fame circumftances.

BUGLE HORN EXERCISE SOUNDINGS.

5. *March*
6. *Trot*
7. *Gallop*
8. *Charge*
9. *Halt*
10. *Retreat*
11. *Rally*
12. *Turn out fkirmifhers*
13. *Skirmifhers ceafe firing*
14. *Call in fkirmifhers*

Thefe foundings are exactly the fame as thofe of the trumpet, in the place of which the bugle horn may be occafionally fubftituted.

Thefe fignals of the trumpet and bugle horn are meant in aid of the voice, but are by no means to be fubftituted for, or prevent the *ordered* words of execution.

The trumpet is always to be confidered as the principal military inftrument for thefe foundings. It more particularly belongs to the line, and the bugle horn to detached parties.

WORDS OF COMMAND.

Comm. Officer.	Squadron Officer.	Divifion Leaders.	*The open Column of Divifions trots paft the General, and again forms in line on the Ground it quitted.*	Obfervations.
*	*		Divifions, left backward wheel!	(*a*) The line may be put threes about, wheeled forward by divifions, halt, front, and drefs.
*	*		March!	
		*	Halt! Drefs!	
*	*		March!	
		*	Left wheel! Forward!	
		*	Left wheel! Forward!	
		*	Eyes Right!	
		*	Carry Swords!	
		*	Slope Swords!	
		*	Eyes Left!	
		*	Left wheel! Forward!	
		*	Left wheel! Forward!	
*	*		Halt!	
*	*		Wheel into line!	
*	*		March!	
		*	Halt! Drefs!	
		*	Eyes Front!	

Comm. Officer.	Squadron Officer.	H. Squa. Officer.	Change of Position on Left Flank, Right thrown back.	Observations.
*	*		Threes about! March! (a)	(a) Left half squadron officer wheels his half squadron the half wheel into the new alignement.
	*		Halt! Dress!	
*	*		Half squadrons—Right quarter wheel! March!	
	*	*	Halt! Dress!	
*	*	*	March!	
		*	Left shoulders forward! Forward! Halt! Front! Halt! Dress! March! Halt! Dress!	

N. B. It is to be considered as an invariable rule, that the caution and words of command, given by the commanding officer previous to every movement, are repeated by the squadron officers to the utmost extent of voice, without which no manœuvre can be executed with precision, as a variety of causes may prevent the commanding officer being heard where the line is extensive.

Comm. Officer.	Squadron Officer.	H. Squa. Officer.	Division Leaders.	*Change of Position in open Column, Left thrown back.*	Observations.
*	*			Divisions—Right wheel! March!	
	*			Halt! Dress!	
			*	Eyes Left!	
*	*			March!	
			*	Right shoulders forward! Forward! (*a*)	(*a*) Repeated by division leaders on arriving at marker 1 and 2
*	*			Halt!—Rear divisions will march into the new direction. (*b*)	(*b*) The squadron in the new alignement wheels into line.
				Threes, Right wheel! March!	
		*		Halt! Dress!	
*	*			March!	
			*	Right shoulders forward! Forward! Halt! Wheel up! Halt! Dress! (*c*)	(*c*) Repeated by division leaders on arriving in the new direction.
*	*			Wheel into line! March!	
		*		Halt! Dress! Eyes front!	

Comn. Officer.	Squadron Officer.	H. Squa. Officer.	*Change of Position on the Right Flank, Left brought forward.*	Observations.
*			Half squadrons—Right quarter wheel! March! (*a*)	(*a*) Right half squadron officer wheels his half squadron into the new alignement.
	*		Half squadrons—Right quarter wheel! March!	
		*	Halt! Dress!	
*	*		March!	
		*	Left shoulders forward! Forward! Halt! Dress! (*b*)	(*b*) Repeated in succession by half squadron officers.
	*		Eyes front!	

| Comm. Officer | Right Wing | | Left Wing | | *Close Column is formed on the Left Half Squadron, marches to its Right, and deploys into Line.* | Observations. |
	Squa. Officer	H. Sq. Officer	Squa. Officer	H. Sq. Officer		
*	*		*		Form close column to the rear of the left half squadron!—Half squadron, Left eighth wheel! March!	
	*		*		Halt! Dress!	
*	*		*		Three's left wheel! March!	
	*		*		Halt! Dress!	
*	*		*		March!	
		*		*	Left shoulders forward! Forward! Halt! Wheel up! Halt! Dress! (*a*)	(*a*) Repeated successively by half squadron officers as they arrive in column.
*					Column—Three's right wheel! March! Halt! Dress! March! Halt! Wheel up! Halt! Dress!	
*					Form line on the right center (or fifth) half squadron—Three's outward wheel!	
	*				Three's right wheel! ⎫ Repeated	
			*		Three's left wheel! ⎬ together.	
*					March! Halt! Dress! March!	
		*		*	Halt! Wheel up! Halt! Dress! March! (*b*)	(*b*) Right wing marches (after wheeling up) by its left, and dresses to that flank. Left wing marches and dresses by its right.
	*		*		Eyes front!	

Comm. Officer.	Squadron Officer.	Division Leaders.	*The Line will countermarch in Column of Divisions.*	Observations.
*	*		Divisions—Right wheel! March	
	*	*	Halt! Dress!	
		*	Eyes left!	
*	*		March! Halt! The divisions will countermarch!	
*	*		To the right file! March!	
		*	(*a*) Left shoulders forward! Forward! Left form!	(*a*) The leading files wheel to the right about after leading out a sufficient distance, to bring the left off its ground before the right arrives to form.

Comm. Officer.	Squadron Officer.	Divifion Leaders.	*The Column will retire by a Flank March of Divifions.*	Obfervations.
*	*		Threes left wheel! March!	
	*		Halt! Drefs!	
*	*		March! Halt! Wheel up!	
	*		Halt! Drefs!	
		*	Eyes right!	
*	*		Right wheel into line! March!	
	*		Halt! Drefs! Eyes front!	

Comm. Officer.	Squadron Officer.	The Line will attack by Squadrons from the Right.	Observations.
*	*	No. 1. March! Trot! Canter! Charge! Halt! (*a*) No. 2. ⎫ No. 3. ⎬ Repeated in succession. No. 4. ⎭	(*a*) Flank markers are turned out (if necessary) by the squadron officer placing himself in the center, and aligning with the serjeant, he moves the squadron up.

Comm. Officer.	Squadron Officer.	The Line will retire in Echellon of Squadrons from the Left.	Observations.
*	*	No. 4. Threes about! March!	
	*	Halt! Dress! March!	
		No. 3. ⎫ No. 2. ⎬ Repeated in succession. (*a*) No. 1. ⎭	(*a*) At a given distance by the commanding officer.
*	*	Form line on the right center (or second) squadron.	
	*	No. 2. ⎫ Halt! Front! Halt!	
		⎧ No. 3. ⎫ Dress!	
	*	⎨ No. 4. ⎬ March! (*b*)	(*b*) No. 1. retires, halts, fronts, and dresses, by No. 2; 3 and 4 advance, halt, and dress, by the same squadron.
		⎩ No. 1. ⎭	

Comm. Officer.	Squadron Officer.	The Line will attack to the Front.	Observations.
*	*	Right center (or second) squadron the squadron of direction—— March! Trot! Canter! Charge! Halt! (a) Dress!	(a) Flank serjeants and squadron officers aligne themselves to correct the line by the directing squadron.

| Comm. Officer. | Right Wing | | Left Wing | | The Line will retire and form two Columns. | Observations. |
	Squa. Officer.	H. Sq. Officer.	Squa. Officer.	H. Sq. Officer.		
*	*				Right wing form column of half squadrons, at quarter distance, behind the adjoining half squadron—Half squadron, left eighth wheel! March!	
	*				Halt! Dress!	
*	*				Three's left wheel! March!	
	*				Halt! Dress!	
*	*				March!	
		*			Halt! Wheel up! Halt! Dress! (a)	(a) A small degree of left shoulders forward is required in the formation of the column.
*	*		*		The column will retire—Three's about! March!	
	*		*		Halt! Dress!	
*	*		*		March! Halt! Front!	
	*		*		Halt! Dress!	
*	*				The column will close to the front—March!	
		*			Halt! Dress!	
*			*		Left squadron, form close column of half squadrons behind the adjoining half squadron—Half squadrons right eighth wheel! March!	
			*		Halt! Dress!	
*			*		Three's right wheel! March!	
			*		Halt! Dress!	
*			*		March!	
				*	Halt! Wheel up! Halt! Dress!	

Comm. Officer.	Right Wing		Left Wing		The Column will attack in Front and Flank.	Observations.
	Squa. Officer.	H. Sq. Officer.	Squa. Officer.	H. Sq. Officer.		
*					Three's outward wheel!	
	*				No. 1, 2, 3, and 4, Three's, right wheel! ⎫	
					⎬ Repeated together.	
			*		No. 7 and 8, Three's left wheel! ⎭	
*	*		*		March!	
	*		*		Halt! Dreſs!	
*	*		*		March!	
				*	No. 7 and 8—Halt! Wheel up! Halt! Dreſs! March! Halt! Dreſs!	
*			*		March!	
		*			No. 4, 3, 2, and 1—Right ſhoulders forward! Forward! Halt! Wheel up! Halt! Dreſs! March! (*a*)	
*		*	*		Trot! Canter! Charge! (*b*) Halt!	(*a*) Repeated by each half ſquadron officer, as they come to the ground on which they are to form. (*b*) The right muſt regulate their paces ſo that both wings may finiſh the charge together

Comm. Officer.	Squadron Officer.	R. H. Sq. Officer.	L. H. Sq. Officer.	The Regiment will retire in two Lines of alternate Half Squadrons from the Right.	Observations.
*	*			Right center (or fifth half squadron) the half squadron of direction!	
	*	*		Threes about! March!	
		*		Halt! Dress!	
*		*		March! (a)	(a) The right wing retires in a circling direction, by bringing left shoulders forward.
*				Halt!	
		*		Halt! Front! Halt! Dress!	
			*	Three's about! March! Halt! Dress! March! Halt! Front! Halt! Dress! (b)	(b) The retreat is continued in this manner till the commanding officer wishes to form line.
		*		Three's about! March! Halt! Dress! March!	
*		*	*	Form line! (c)	(c) On the half squadrons most retired.
		*		Halt! Front! Halt! Dress!	
	*			Eyes front!	

www.ingramcontent.com/pod-product-compliance
Lightning Source LLC
LaVergne TN
LVHW091300080426
835510LV00007B/339